This edition
has been limited to
2,500 numbered copies
of which this is
No. **653**

Heyday of the
Somerset & Dorset Railway

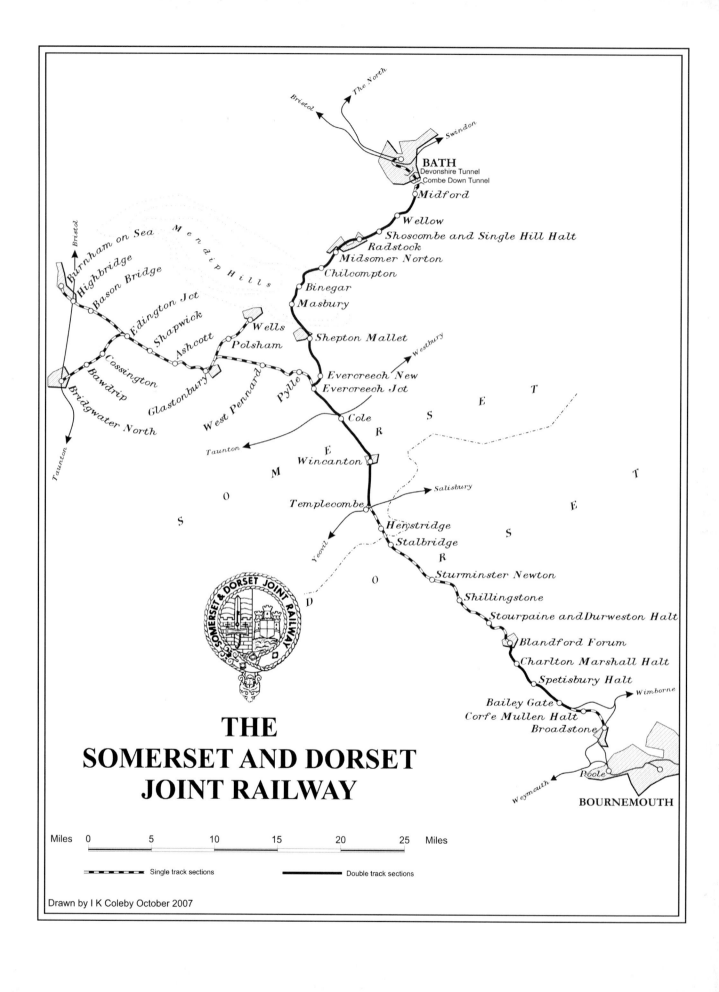

THE
SOMERSET AND DORSET
JOINT RAILWAY

The North

Bristol

Swindon

BATH
Devonshire Tunnel
Combe Down Tunnel

Midford

Wellow

Shoscombe and Single Hill Halt
Radstock
Midsomer Norton

Chilcompton

Binegar

Masbury

Shepton Mallet

Bristol

Burnham on Sea

Highbridge

Bason Bridge

Mendip Hills

Edington Jct

Shapwick

Wells

Ashcott

Polsham

Cossington

Bawdrip

Glastonbury

West Pennard

Pylle

Westbury

Evercreech New
Evercreech Jct

Bridgwater North

Taunton

Cole

Taunton

Wincanton

Salisbury

Templecombe

Yeovil

Henstridge

Stalbridge

Sturminster Newton

Shillingstone

Stourpaine and Durweston Halt

Blandford Forum

Charlton Marshall Halt

Spetisbury Halt

Bailey Gate
Corfe Mullen Halt
Broadstone

Wimborne

Poole

Weymouth

BOURNEMOUTH

SOMERSET & DORSET JOINT RAILWAY

| Miles | 0 | | 5 | | 10 | | 15 | | 20 | | 25 | | Miles |

Single track sections

Double track sections

Drawn by I K Coleby October 2007

Heyday of the Somerset & Dorset Railway

Alan & Christine Hammond

Millstream Books

*This book is dedicated to all the men and women, past and present, who worked on the Somerset & Dorset Railway.
They were the legends that made this line into one of the most talked about and loved railways from yesteryear.
They had pride in their railway, with many generations of families following each other to work on the line.
For many of them this was not just a job, but a way of life that they enjoyed and treasured.*

*Also special mention must go to Roy Pitman of the SDRT, who was the driving force back in the 1980s,
supported by his wife Mona, in organising the staff reunions at Washford, which he did for over 20 years.
These events brought together former workmates and are still an important date in the calendar for S&D staff today.*

A reunion at Washford for S&D staff in 1989. The photograph includes Roy Pitman on the left and S&D railway men and woman, Betty Spiller, Ron Gray, Fred and Percy Parsons, Arthur King, George Dyer, Keith Barrett, Johnny Walker, Eric Elford, Reg Brewer, Reg Darke, Ted Lambert, Albert (Dickie) Bird, Den Matthews, David Hughes, Fred Fisher and Wilf Jeans. (*Mona Pitman collection*)

First published in 2008 by
Millstream Books, 18 The Tyning, Bath BA2 6AL

Set in Times New Roman and printed in Great Britain by
The Amadeus Press, Cleckheaton, West Yorkshire

© Alan & Christine Hammond 2008

ISBN 978 0 948975 83 7

British Library Cataloguing-in-Publication Data:
a catalogue record for this book is available from the British Library

Foreword

My interest in railways started at the age of 15 when I was invited by the Royal Army Service Corps to come and drive a locomotive at their training centre in Hampshire called Longmoor Halt. The locomotive had a train attached to it. I drove it with great panache, but brought it to a stop at the next station so smoothly and gently that none of the passengers (the train was full) got out and I had to jiggle the regulator until they realised we had arrived and then they all put their newspapers down and emerged rather sheepishly.

On another occasion I went down to pay a visit to David Shepherd's very impressive private line at Cranmore, the East Somerset Railway, where I drove his magnificent *Black Prince*. You have to be quite careful, with all that power, how you accelerate: wheelspin is not difficult to induce, even without leaves on the line.

More recently I was accorded the great distinction of having a Great Western Trains railway engine (or High Speed Train Power Cars as they are called nowadays) named after me, at Bristol Temple Meads. After the naming ceremony I travelled in the driver's cab of this beautiful, dark blue, shiny beast all the way to Paddington. I was not allowed to drive it (union rules) but I sat in the simulator at Bristol instead and cruised all over the south of England undisturbed. What a feeling of power!

I am off soon to drive a Soviet-era steam engine on the Trans-Siberian line out of Moscow, pulling a brand new 20-coach train that has been built by a British company. Having cut my teeth on so many locomotives in the past, I hope I pass the test.

This new book, *Heyday of the Somerset and Dorset Railway*, has been put together with meticulous care and includes a number of people's memories of this line from the mid-1940s until 1966, when the line closed. Together with the excellent photographs, it stands as the best possible record of this splendid railway, and I thoroughly commend it.

Prince Michael of Kent
2007

Introduction and Acknowledgements

I would like to thank everybody who has bought my previous books. I am most grateful for your support and encouragement over the years. This is my ninth book on the Somerset & Dorset Railway and as you can see my wife Christine is co-author. She has had a tremendous input into the book with her photograph and computer skills and fully deserves her co-authorship.

We feel this publication is three books in one, with the Somerset Central, Dorset Central and the Bath Extension, that made up the Somerset & Dorset Railway. With the Somerset Central and the Dorset Central we have added the various extensions to the two lines. These three sections of the line had distinctive characteristics, from the Somerset Levels on the branch, to the Mendip Hills towards Bath and the agricultural land of Dorset that took you to the coast at Bournemouth.

When meeting people for the first time, the question I am always asked the most is 'Where do you keep getting the material from?' The Somerset & Dorset Railway is a very popular railway and has a special relationship with many people from all over the world. Over the years people like Ivo Peters, Robin Atthill and Mike Arlett have graced us with their books and films. A major factor are the preservation groups of the S&D Trust at Washford, the S&D Heritage Trust at Midsomer Norton and the North Dorset Railway Trust at Shillingstone as well as the train rides along the trackbed of the old Dorset, at Gartell Light Railway near Templecombe.

More recently the excellent 40th anniversary DVD of the S&D by Mike Arlett and hopefully my last book, *Celebration of the Somerset & Dorset Railway*, have brought this railway to the attention of many people. This has stimulated interest and has brought back memories for people who either travelled or worked on the line. Since this anniversary I have had hundreds of new photographs sent to me and the offer of many stories of the line. This new book hopefully continues this love affair with the railway, containing a wealth of brand new photographs and memories.

We have also been fortunate that a number of well-known people have very kindly given us their own personal memories of railways. It is nice to know that there is still a great deal of interest in our steam heritage from people from all walks of life.

You cannot hope to put together a book like this without lots of help and advice. We have been very lucky to have had all this from many people, which has made the book truly a team effort.

Extended and sincere thanks go to our publisher Tim Graham, who has again done a great job in designing the book.

Our very profound thanks go to Prince Michael of Kent for writing the foreword. The Prince has had a lifelong fascination with railways and is a firm supporter of preserved railways.

Thanks also go to Michael Eavis, CBE, who most willingly and enthusiastically gave us his memories of the S&D; to Tony Christie who very kindly gave us nostalgic memories of his early trainspotting days at his home station and beyond; and to Gary Brooker, MBE, who remembers travelling by steam at a young age and collecting locomotive numbers, which was all part of growing up in the 1950s.

Our very good friend, former S&D fireman Keith Barrett has been of great assistance and help in all aspects of the book including the use of many photographs from his personal collection. A big thank-you goes to John Simms, who has written a marvellous history of the line in his own unique fashion, and to Andy Moon who has given us great advice and help with his vast knowledge of the S&D. Tim Deacon has again supported us with the names of many railway staff for which we are most grateful.

For their specific and important contributions to this book we owe a particular debt of gratitude to the contributors of the stories; Richard Gunning, John Tooze, Ron Jeans, David Herring, John Baker, Tony Rossiter, Gordon King, Ken Padfield, Brian Davis, John Eaton, Bill Pike and Charlie Robinson; we couldn't have done it without you.

Special mention must go to Peter Morton, Paul Strong and Alan Mitchard who have allowed us open access to their photographs. Many thanks also go to the other photographers who have allowed us to use their pictures.

We are very grateful to Ian Coleby who has drawn the superb map of the S&D specially for the book and also for proof-reading the manuscript. A very big thanks, too, to the other proof readers: Roy Pitman, Allan Stanistreet, Keith Barrett, Richard Derry and Graham Hooper.

Many others have given their time, help and advice including The Somerset & Dorset Railway Trust, The Somerset and Dorset Railway Heritage Trust, North Dorset Railway Trust, Sturminster Newton Museum Society, Pete Collings, Pauline Keen, George Tucker, Ralph Holden, Arthur Turner, Nancy Holmes, Chris Cooke, Rita Pettet, Roger Raisey, Steve Case, Helmut Eckardt, Connie Miles, Vince Henderson, Chris & George Hitchcock, John Yeo, Andrew Padfield, Andy Viles, Roger Joanes, Wally Moon, Brenda Griffin, Sean Fitzgerald, Lesley Miles, John Stamp, Bob Downes, Richard Dagger, Monty Morris, Ivor Willshire, Percy Parsons, Norman Cook, Frank Kemp, Bob Weaver, Barry Andrews, Brian & Len Taylor, Wally Arnott, Max Shore, Rita Smart, Mary Haines, David Strawbridge, Maureen Carroll, John Pearce, Ian Matthews, Stuart Mullins, Francis Pook, Vic Freak, Roy Cox, Jim Milton, Jack Powis, Norman Hawkes, David Milton, Gwyn Rogers, Brian Harding, M.K. Lewis, Norman Ashman, Geoff & Mary Clacy, Dr. Peter Darke, Gordon Scammel, David Sheldon, Peter Hitchcock, Paul Fry, Jim Randall, Chris Nevard, David Walden, Keith Baker and Chris Osment.

As many photographs are from people's private collections a reader may well recognise a photograph that they took themselves. We offer our apologies in advance for not being able to credit you in person.

It is a sad fact that many of the former staff have now passed away. Since the last book we have lost Bernard Ware, Fred Fisher, Eric Miles, Freda Box, Alan Larcombe, Keith Conibeer, Roy Paulley, Alan Cox, Pat Holmes, Charlie Watkins and Leo Elkins.

Christine and Alan Hammond with actress Su Pollard who is holding their previous book, *Return Ticket to Minehead*, to which she contributed. (*Steve Guscott*)

The Somerset Central Railway
and the Extensions to Burnham-on-Sea and Wells

John Simms

The Somerset Levels was the area that gave the ancient English county its name. An area of flat ground crossed by rivers that meander sluggishly once they come down from the surrounding hills, it has throughout its history been prone to flooding in the winter and it was the 'Summer folk' who brought their cattle and stock down to graze in the longer days of summer whose memory is commemorated.

Travel on the moors has traditionally been difficult. Our bronze and iron age forebears lived on islands amongst the lakes and reeds and got about by means of boats and some beautifully engineered wooden causeways. Boats continued to be used into medieval times and Glastonbury saw small ships coming to it from the Bristol Channel. But the slow meandering flow of the Brue and the other rivers, such as the Parrett and the Tone, meant that all water channels were prone to silting and it was a constant battle to move about.

By the early 19th century the old ecclesiastical centre of Glastonbury and its neighbouring village of Street had begun to see industrial growth with shoemaking and sheepskins prominent. This meant a growing demand to get goods out and raw materials in and so the Glastonbury Canal was built. Although built in the last part of the 'Canal Age' it was not a great success. Money ran short, construction was skimped and as water leaked into the marshland the surrounding peat expanded and the depth of the canal was reduced.

Alternatives were sought. The Bristol and Exeter Railway was built in the 1840s as an effective extension of Brunel's broad-gauge Great Western Railway and skirted the Levels as it ran down through Highbridge and Bridgwater. The Somerset Central Railway was promoted as a broad-gauge branch of this line to link the Bristol Channel coast at Highbridge with Glastonbury, and not much else in-between.

On 28 August 1854 Glastonbury welcomed its first trains. Having got to a town noted for its ancient (if ruined) Abbey and having been promoted by non-conformist families such as the shoemaking Clarks the Somerset Central got an urge to meet the higher church and turned across another section of the Levels to the cathedral city of Wells which it reached in 1859. The trains were running and connection had been made

with the outside world, and had history followed its usual pattern the Somerset Central would eventually have become part of the Great Western.

In fact extension was next planned from Glastonbury to Bruton where it would have joined the Wilts, Somerset & Weymouth, another broad-gauge line. Track was being laid and earthworks for the junction at Bruton where the meeting was to be effected were being made. And then one of the great engineering dreams of the time took a hand. This was a link between the Bristol and English Channels that would alleviate the need for ships to make the hazardous journey round Lands End.

Ship canals had been proposed but never built, but now with the Dorset Central Railway making its way north from Poole, a combination with the Somerset Central would make the connection. The problem with this was that as the Dorset Central was standard gauge, the Somerset Central would have to change its gauge and the Bristol and Exeter would not be able to work it. Nonetheless the combination went ahead in 1862.

The first extension from Highbridge to Burnham opened in 1858 and the new Somerset and Dorset Railway finally offered the Channel to Channel link. Unfortunately the completion of this particular dream coincided with improvements in marine technology. Iron-hulled ships with steam engines were able to negate most of the perils of Lands End and thus the Somerset and Dorset Railway became a bucolic line with its trains running through lovely countryside but without much by way of traffic.

And so it was in 1874 that the S&D extended from Evercreech to Bath through the Somerset Coalfield. Once the Bath Extension was open the original Somerset Central became a branch line and remained that way until final closure in 1966.

A final line to Bridgwater was built from Edington in 1890 but this did not develop into a major source of traffic, useful though it was for some businesses in Bridgwater seeking alternative routes for their goods.

Most trains began their journeys at Evercreech (now known as Evercreech Junction) but some came up from Templecombe, running through Cole along the way. The atmosphere settled down to a pattern that felt as though it would go on forever. Small engines hauled two or three coaches under acres of sky with distant views of the Polden, Mendip and Quantock Hills to remind the traveller that the train had not gone off the edge of the world. Only the excursion trains to the seaside at Burnham produced long lines of carriages, many of them antiques that had not turned a wheel since the summer before. The engines were older, smaller ones, the freight trains shunted in and out of the goods yards at the stations along the way and the timetable barely altered year after year. On the Wells branch a single coach was enough for passengers making the short trip to and from Glastonbury. Bridgwater could also accommodate its travellers in one vehicle.

For most of the route the stations were remote, positioned to give the easiest engineering when the line was built. Even now (2008) West Pennard station stands remote at one end of the village it served, an example of why when the buses came in the 1920s the passengers for Glastonbury deserted the trains. At Bason Bridge there was always plenty of milk traffic and Highbridge had the railway workshops until 1930 plus small coastal ships at Highbridge Wharf but bustle was rare and changes of ownership barely impacted as the Somerset and Dorset became part of the LMS, then British Railways Southern Region and finally Western Region. As one generation of old engines wore out the next was drafted in and when some modern machines did appear the timetable stayed as relaxed as ever.

Other things stayed unchangeable too. Water for the Crossing Keepers' houses along the line was carried out in a milk churn on the engines and it all seemed so timeless that the late John Betjeman came to make a film called *Branchline Railway*.

But passenger numbers had faded to a handful and freight kept moving away to lorries, so poets with film crews would never be enough to keep the line open. Wells lost its Somerset and Dorset trains in 1951 and the last one out of Bridgwater departed in 1952. Finally in March 1966 it all came to an end, except for the milk traffic between Bason Bridge and Highbridge which lingered on until 1972.

The resemblance between the line and a miniature painting helped to make for a special atmosphere. The lack of hurry and the quiet nature of operations meant that the staff, the passengers and the freight customers all knew each other well. Indeed in many cases they were related. And it is the memories of this atmosphere that Alan Hammond has been recording for many years to give an insight into a world that seems much more remote in time than two generations ago.

An overgrown platform at Burnham-on-Sea sums up the rural nature of the Branch. Excited children look on as an excursion train in the 1950s is about to leave with 3F No.43248 at the helm. (*Alan Powell*)

9

(*above*) The delights of early summer enhance this view of 1P No.1406 going bunker first with two coaches at Burnham-on-Sea, c.1948. (*Joe Moss/R.S. Carpenter collection*)

(*below*) A Fox Walker Saddle Tank No.1505 simmers gently at the terminus of Burnham-on-Sea in the 1930s. The footplate crew and another member of staff pose for the photographer. (*Keith Barrett collection*)

(*above*) A 3F with a service train for Templecombe is about to set sail from Burnham-on-Sea in 1954. The gentleman wearing the smart blazer is Francis Pook. This photograph reminds me of my own youth in Essex. With my good friend Bob Kent we would stand by an engine like the young lads in this photograph and soak up the atmosphere of steam. (*Alan Powell*)

(*below*) A lazy afternoon in high summer at Burnham-on-Sea in 1958 as 3F No.43194 gets ready to take out a local passenger service train. (*R.M. Casserley*)

(*above*) Staff from one of the workshops at Highbridge in the early 1900s. The works were opened by the Somerset & Dorset Railway in 1862. In its heyday well over 300 people worked there making or repairing everything that the railway needed, from locos to carriages to boilers. (*SDRT collection*)

(*left*) Two tradesmen and probably an apprentice at Highbridge Works in the early 1900s. It was certainly a family concern as generations of families followed each other into the various railway departments. (*SDRT collection*)

(*above*) A close up view of Ernest Pitcher who worked in the 1940s at Highbridge Wharf as a crane driver. (*SDRT collection*)

(*below*) A serene photograph of a lady at Highbridge ticket office. We would love to know who she is and when it was taken? (*Authors' collection*)

(*above*) Signalman George Dewfall photographed at Highbridge in 1946. George joined the S&D in 1894; he later became the bobby at Highbridge B box for many years. He gave over 50 years' service to the Somerset & Dorset. (*Roy Cox collection*)

(*below*) Pictured here by the water tower at Highbridge is Johnson 0-6-0 3F No.43218. Looking out of the cab is senior driver on the branch, Charlie King. (*Keith Barrett collection*)

John Baker & Tony Rossiter

I met John and Tony at Washford at one of the S&D reunions. I was fortunate enough to have my tape recorder with me as they reminisced about their days as young firemen at Highbridge in the 1960s. These are a few of their memories for you to enjoy.

Tony: In 1961 I started work as a fireman at Highbridge. The roster covered about six turns of duty. The first turn was to work the 7.00am passenger from Highbridge to Evercreech Junction and return with the 8.15am from Evercreech Junction to Highbridge, then out with the 9.45am to Templecombe and then return with the 1.15pm from Evercreech. Second turn was to travel to Evercreech on the cushions on the 9.45am passenger, normally on 4F No.44560, and work back to Highbridge Wharf with the 11.00am goods, shunting all the stations *en route*. Third turn work was the 4.00pm from Highbridge to Evercreech Junction and return back to Highbridge. Fourth turn work was the 4.15pm milk tanks from Bason Bridge to Templecombe, then travel home on the cushions on the 9.25pm passenger from Evercreech Junction. Fifth turn was to work the 7.10pm passenger from Highbridge to Evercreech Junction and return with the 9.25pm from Evercreech Junction and the final turn was shunting goods at Highbridge, Bason Bridge and Burnham.

The driver I fired to was Ronald (Chummy) Andrews. Chummy was all right on the main line but he didn't like shunting. Once we got to Glastonbury he would find somebody to talk to and he would be off. So at 17 years of age I would do the shunting which I really enjoyed. Chummy was a good old boy and it has been mentioned many times before that he was a real S&D character. One of his hobbies was beekeeping. When it was time for a bit of food on the footplate he would try and swap one of his honey sarnies for one of your ham ones. He liked his drop of cider and when we were up the Junction at Evercreech we would have a quick glass at the *Railway Hotel* and a chat with the other railwaymen. He was a very good driver and there was never a dull moment.

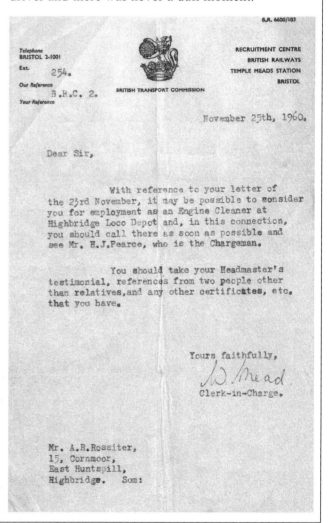

The advertisement in the *Bristol Evening Post* in November 1960 to which Tony Rossiter responded and the reply he received.

Getting ready to leave at Highbridge East is a rather weather-beaten Ivatt class 2 Tank No.41283 with a train of milk tanks for Bason Bridge. (*Keith Barrett collection*)

Another driver was Harry Pearce (known as Sitting Bull); for whatever reason he didn't like opening the regulator. One night on the last train at Edington Burtle we were there for 50 minutes blowing up steam, we couldn't get enough steam for the trip to Highbridge. He just wouldn't open the regulator. He would just be sitting there in the corner smoking his Woodbine while I was working as hard as I could with sweat dripping off me. He would say: 'When you are ready we will move'.

The track from Edington to Highbridge was very flat; the worst bit of the line was Pylle Bank. I recall approaching the Junction from West Pennard with the milk train one day with 12 tanks on from Highbridge. You knew you had a load on near the bank especially when you had a 'Mickey Mouse' tank engine which we used to call the Ivatts. No.41242 was the worst, no one could get her to steam. The best one was 41296 with a tall chimney.

John: I started on the railway in 1962 and was sent to Bath Green Park for training as a fireman; this lasted for about six weeks. The school room was an old coach jacked up on sleepers. We were under the watchful eye of Mr. Arthur MacCarthy who smoked about 60 cigarettes in the eight hours we were there. As I was not allowed to do overtime I had to sign on at Highbridge loco shed, walk to the station, catch a train to Bath Spa and then walk through the town to Bath Green Park. After school it was a train to Temple Meads where a goods train was waiting to take me to Highbridge to drop me off.

I would often ride on the footplate and have a go with the shovel. I used to fire to old George Wheadon a real character; he had his leg badly damaged by a train accident. Old George would say to you if you were down the pan and you couldn't get any steam: 'If you don't get this thing going I'll take my wooden leg off and put it in the firebox to get some steam up'.

Another driver was Bill May. He was a real gentleman and he took me under his wing, but he did have his moments, especially when I was giving him a bit of back chat as a 16-year-old. One day we were on a 4F and old Bill was having a quiet moment sitting on the seat on the regulator rack. I turned around and said to him: 'You look like a bald parrot up there Bill'. He took it all in good fun and he was great to work with. Many years later when Bill sadly died and his funeral was taking place, a steam engine went through Highbridge at the same time, and the crew whistled up. A great tribute to a great railwayman. Another time with Bill, we were on a passenger train on the branch and it was late at night. The motive power was an Ivatt Tankie; as we were going along there was a hell of a bang and the old engine rocked from side to side. I was kicking the door out to get off as I thought we were off the rails. Bill said: 'Hang on we have only broken a fish plate' We smelt flesh all the way to Highbridge. When we arrived, the ladder on the bunker was all bent up. Bill said: 'We don't know nothing, do we?' When we run round the shed with the coach on, you could see what we had hit, a cow was cooking up on the ledge of the ashpan.

Tony: When we were on a goods train we would always see the ganger at Pylle Woods for our Christmas trees. We would stick them on the tender and bring them home; also if we wanted any pea sticks for the garden we would do the same thing.

I remember a trip we did in the bad winter of 1963. We were up the Junction waiting for the Bournemouth train to come in. It was late in coming so we visited the *Railway Hotel*, three times. Eventually it came in about midnight. My driver was Clarence Rawles who lived at Shepton Mallet. There was a set of men who used to ride home on the cushions on the Bath train after bringing in the milk train. As Clarence lived at Shepton and the snow was really bad, one of the drivers Ron Sandercock said he would never get home from Highbridge and he would take the train down the branch for him, which was a nice gesture.

Ron came on the footplate with me and we set sail in the snow to go down the branch. We got down to Glastonbury all right, then headed for Ashcott. We got to the reverse curve, then before Ashcott, the distant signal told us the crossing gates were open. Ron opened the regulator and come thundering around the curve. When we got to the straight we could see the red light in the middle of the track, so we shut off steam and put the loco into reverse. It was no good, the wheels just picked up and we went straight through the two line gates and smashed them to smithereens. We finished up stopping at the goods yard.

Our guard Jimmy Yelling got out of his van and walked back to the station and hollered up to the bedroom window. Archie Atwell stuck his head out of the window half asleep and shouted back down

to Jimmy: 'I got tired of waiting for you, you let yourself through the gates'. Jimmy shouted back: 'Let ourselves through the gates, we've done that all right, no problem, but you are going to need a bloody new pair'. What had happened with the distant signal arm is that lots of snow had gathered on the arm and made it drop down. We were summoned to Bristol regarding this accident and Ron got two days' suspension and I got one day. Later I married Archie's daughter Janet and we now live at Ashcott's old station.

A letter sent to Tony Rossiter by Dr. Beeching in 1961.

John and Tony: None of the crossing keepers' cottages had running water so we used to deliver the water churns on the engine. At Pennard Lane Crossing we always got a hot cup of tea from the crossing keeper Evelyn Curtis and old Bill May would always call her 'Mother'. All the drivers would let you put the churns in the cab except Charlie King who would never have them in the cab. You had to put them up the front of the smokebox. Sometimes coming off the branch a pheasant wrapped itself around the buffer beam. By the time you knew about it somebody would have spotted it and they would have it in their pot. We used to stop on the goods train and pick up some mushrooms in the fields; with egg and bacon on the shovel it was a mouth-watering breakfast.

John: Being young lads we were always getting up to mischief, the trouble was that if you did something wrong at Highbridge, by the time you reached Templecombe everybody knew about it. We used to have a morning turn on shed at Highbridge. At midday you had to go to Bason Bridge and shunt some milk tanks. Well we were young and we wanted to get off to go down to Burnham-on-Sea. In the old signalbox there were phones you could pick up and talk from box to box. I would pick the phone up when the signalman popped out of the box and I'd ring the porter at Bason

Bridge and ask: 'Do you want any tanks today?' Most times they did, but I used to say: 'Well we want to go out later and we don't want to come there'. If the porter was a good old boy he would say: 'Well forget it, we'll do it at 4.00pm'. Of course you were not on duty then. You would say to your driver: 'They've just rang up from Bason Bridge and they don't want any tanks today'. The old driver would say to you: 'Well done'.

When the driver booked on in the morning he would see what fireman he had on the sheet. He couldn't confirm that was the fireman because we would chop around ourselves if we wanted to do something else, but we always made sure that one of us was there.

We used to have a bit of fun with the signalmen, they would sometimes torment you. In the summer time you would have your short-sleeved shirt on and when you caught the tablet you would get black grease all up your arm. What we used to do then was, on the way back, to put the tablet on the manifold and warm the bugger up. When the signalman caught it, you would watch him jump up in the air.

When the ash heap got too big they used to ask for volunteers to load the ashes into a 16-ton truck; two firemen were paid 16 hours each. This was not an easy task and not many wanted the work. The job got worse as the truck began to fill up which was easy if it was windy as you had to put the ashes over the top. Tony and I decided that there must be an easier way to do this dirty job. We realised that a tractor and loader would help. So when this job came up we quickly volunteered our services. The other firemen were quite pleased about this. We borrowed the tractor and loader from a local farmer for the price of 40 Player cigarettes and did the job in two hours. We got very confident at doing this job until one shift. We were going out on the Sunday so decided to do the job on the Saturday night. We arrived with the tractor and loader and started work when all of a sudden Jim Hayes, who was the steamraiser, came running out thinking the noise was a steam engine running away. Whilst loading the truck that night the front wheel got stuck in the ash pit; moving back and forth the back wheel then got stuck and by then the tractor was nearly lying on its side. Luckily for us a Mickey Mouse Tank No.41296 was behind us in steam. We quickly drove the engine up to the pit, put the pricker bar under the tractor's draw bar and the handle over the lamp bracket. We then reversed slowly and pulled the tractor along the pit and up the steps. After a quick

December, 1964. BR.29621. W.R. TELEPHONE CIRCUIT NO. 788. HIGHBRIDGE AND BURNHAM-ON-SEA - EVERCREECH.	
STATION	CALL
Highbridge & B. Office	1 - 6
" East "C" Box.	2 - 1
" R. & M. Depot	4 - 2
Bason Bdge. Office	2 - 2
" " Sidings G.F.	2-1 -2
Edington Burtle Office.	2
Shapwick Box.	4
Ashcott Box	2-2-1
Glastonbury & S. Box.	3
Pennard Lane Crossing	2 - 3
Stean Bow Crossing	1 - 2
Cockmill Crossing	1
Elbow Corner Crossing	1 - 3
Evercreech Jt. North Box.	6
⌀Evercreech Jct. Office	1 -4-1
⌀ Switch to Bath - Highbridge Circuit W.R. 728.	

17

inspection of the tractor, which was okay, we then finished loading and enjoyed a cup of tea with Jim. I drove the tractor back to the farmer about 2.00am with the 40 Players left under the seat. I wonder if this was the only agricultural tractor to have been pulled by a Mickey Mouse Tank.

John & Tony: Some of our workmates that we haven't mentioned included firemen Derek Criddle (Fizzle), Mike Lewis (Gunner), Bill Conibeer (Connie), Roger Parker (Percy), whose father Jim was stationmaster at Bason Bridge, George Stent and Terry Fry. Drivers were Maurice Cook, Les Warren and Jack Foster. There were fitters Phil Owen and Cyril Burrows (Captain),

carriage and wagon examiner Derek Jones (Slinger), steamraiser Jim Hayes (his nickname was 'Frigger' because when he filled in the accident report book he would say: 'Tripped over this friggering, friggering stray cat and this lump of coal fell on my friggering, friggering toe'; everything was friggering.) By the way our nicknames were 'Bronco' (John) and 'Dr. Rossi' (Tony).

The Somerset & Dorset Railway gave us the best days of our life and if it was still here today we would be back on it as firemen. Everybody knew each other and you never used to moan about going to work, you used to look forward to it. We know it has been said many times before but it was one big happy family.

(*above*) A fine side view of a pair of Johnson 0-4-4Ts, Nos. 13 and 14A, waiting their turn to go into service at Highbridge on 30 May 1929. (*H.C. Casserley*)

(*below*) An 80-year-old photograph brings the nostalgic days of the Somerset & Dorset Railway back to life at Highbridge, as an unidentified 1P 0-4-4T leaves the station with a Burnham to Evercreech train. (*Keith Barrett collection*)

(*above*) A rare wartime photograph of 1P No.1397 shunting at Highbridge Wharf on 3 March 1945. We wonder what the full name is of the Grimsby Company on the side of the wagon? (*WSRA collection*)

(*below*) A vintage view of class 2251 0-6-0 No.3206 about to leave Highbridge for a trip over the Somerset levels with a passenger train. (*Authors' collection*)

What a great photograph of Buncombe steam rollers taken at Highbridge in 1926. The Company had a steam business in Highbridge. Norman Buncombe is third from the left in this picture. (*Pete Collings collection*)

Platform 5 on a rather damp and dismal day at Highbridge station. Driver Les Warren is on the footplate of the 0-6-0 and his fireman Keith Conibeer is on the outside of the cab. (*Keith Barrett collection*)

(*above*) Waiting to leave Highbridge East signalbox in October 1964 is a Collett class 2251 with a train load of milk tanks for Bason Bridge. Arriving with a short freight from Evercreech Junction is the same class No.2217. (*Paul Strong*)

(*below*) The 19-lever Highbridge East A signalbox which controlled the A38 main road to the West Country before the M5 was built. The box closed to traffic in 1965. (*Keith Barrett collection*)

(*above*) Looking across the River Brue one is rewarded with this superb view of a mixed train headed by a Collett 0-6-0 No.3210 at Bason Bridge with a stopping train from Evercreech to Highbridge in May 1963. (*R.E. Toop*)

(*below*) Ivatt Tanks Nos. 41283 and 41249 prepare to leave Bason Bridge with a milk train on 6 March 1966, the last official steam working on the S&D. A permanent way man appears to be cleaning points by the last milk tank. (*Keith Barrett collection*)

Time stands still as the undergrowth has taken over Edington Burtle station, c.1965. Seen from the old Bridgwater platform is the *Tom Mogg Inn* on the left and behind the canopy is Station House. (*R.M. Casserley*)

Out of all the photographs we have seen of Edington Junction (changed to Edington Burtle in 1953) we have never seen so many people on the platform. Could it be a special occasion as they are nearly all dressed in their Sunday best? If you look closely the signalman is posing for the picture as well, c.1910. (*SDRT collection*)

(*above*) Ambling past the crossing gates at Edington Junction is class 3F No.43248 with a train for Highbridge. The cows on the right are not stirred from their grazing by the loud loco; they have heard and seen it all before. (*SDRT collection*)

(*below*) This photograph affords a fine view of class 2251 0-6-0 No.3210 on an Evercreech to Highbridge local at Edington Burtle in November 1964. (*Paul Strong*)

(*above*) Taken in the early 1950s at Cossington station is 3F No.43194 with a two-coach train for Bridgwater. A member of the public appears to be getting off the train, but we can't see any staff on the platform to greet him. Staff who have worked at this station include Frank Staddon (whose brother Reg worked as a shunter at Bath Green Park), Will Locke, George Pepperall and Fred Parsons. (*Maurice Dean/Richard Dagger collection*)

(*left*) Seen here are five permanent way men on the Bridg-water to Edington branch in the 1930s. It was a tough life for tough men on the moor, especially in the winter months. From left to right are ganger Gilbert Grant, unknown, Frank Groves, Frank (Nackie) Lee and Sam Rice. (*Percy Parsons collection*)

Two marvellous photographs from the 1930s taken at Cossington cutting looking towards Stone End Crossing, which can just be seen in the distance on the right. The five permanent way men, who include Frank Groves and Gilbert Grant, are posing on the hand trolley. These men looked after the line from Edington to Bridgwater. In the picture below the gang are slewing the track. Gilbert is giving instructions to his men but they have only eyes for the photographer. If you look very closely on the right a train has just passed Stone End Crossing. (*Percy Parsons collection*)

A quite rare photograph of Bridgwater North S&D with 3F No.43194 shunting a mixed train in the 1950s. In the middle of the photo is the station. What a pity it is now a supermarket. (*Maurice Dean/Richard Dagger collection*)

David Herring

My family moved to the centre of Bridgwater in 1953 and the Docks Branch of the old GWR became my childhood playground. I clearly remember my fascination, as an eight-year-old, watching the new connection being laid one weekend between the branch and the old S&D sidings, following the final closure of the line from Bridgwater North to Edington Junction. I believe that after that new connection was laid it was the Bridgwater Docks shunter (ex Cardiff Railway 0-4-0ST loco No.1338, and affectionately known by us trainspotters as 'Coffee Pot') that most often serviced the S&D sidings.

Just off the S&D route but well worth showing is 0-4-0ST No.1338 (nicknamed 'Coffee Pot') carrying out shunting duties at Bridgwater Docks in 1960. (*Arthur Garry/Dr. Peter Darke*)

From the same period I also remember walking along the strangely deserted Bristol Road with my younger sister early one Sunday morning to watch the removal of the girder bridge carrying the S&D over the main A38 road. In those years I would often roam around the S&D sidings and eventually took some of my earliest railway photos there.

One other childhood S&D memory is of Highbridge Church Street Level Crossing, and seeing a steam engine on the Burnham-on-Sea branch waiting at the gates for the road traffic, rather than the other way round.

With my teenage trainspotting friends (including Mike Perry and Brian Harding), I was never 'off-duty' and a number of us who belonged to the History Club

at the local grammar school would always look for the railway interest on the end-of-term trips, much to the disapproval of the accompanying teachers. One vivid memory is of walking around Masbury Castle, supposedly to learn the details of this ancient hill-fort, and being much more interested in the clear view of Masbury S&D station far below.

Mike Perry and I decided to cycle to Evercreech Junction to do some trainspotting one day in our summer holidays in 1962, and I'll never forget my surprise at discovering how far it is from Bridgwater. Nevertheless, the day spent at that wonderful station is another precious part of my very happy childhood memories.

One of the boys in my form at grammar school was Charlie Yelling, who lived at the old station house at Cossington, and whose father Jimmy was a guard on the S&D.

I only travelled on the S&D twice. First, on 17 February 1964 while I was still an impecunious schoolboy, when I managed to save up enough to make a round trip. I caught the 09.45 from Highbridge to Templecombe, then the 11.48 to Bournemouth West, and finally the 13.10 from Bournemouth to Bristol Temple Meads, returning to Bridgwater on the main line. Then, later, I made the trip from Highbridge to Glastonbury on 5 March 1966, the last day of passenger traffic, and returned on the very last service train that evening.

On leaving school in February 1964 following my 'A' levels, I was fortunate to be chosen to join British Rail's Railway Studentship Scheme, a junior management training project. The programme developed for me required me to first work for eight months at Bridgwater Station – Goods, Passenger and Parcels sections – and there I met several ex-S&D personnel, including Will Locke and Joyce Fear.

I had a real sense of foreboding when I reported to Mr. Saunders, the stationmaster, on the first morning. It hadn't been many years previous when several of us young trainspotters were caught running across the sidings near the station. We were hauled to see Mr. Saunders by, I believe, Mr. Locke. After a stern dressing down Mr. Saunders took our names and addresses and informed us he never wanted to see any of us on the railway again. To my relief he appeared to have completely forgotten the incident when as a student I presented myself to him for work.

An abiding memory of the time I spent at the goods depot was of Christmas Eve 1964, when a consignment of Christmas turkeys (dead!) arriving by rail had earlier gone astray. They eventually turned up during the afternoon, long after most delivery staff had gone home, and Jack Warren, the yard foreman, was running around in circles trying to arrange delivery of these Christmas dinners. Even now I can see Sylvia Hucker (later Hawkins), a clerk in the goods office, valiantly loading boxed turkeys on the back of her moped for local delivery.

It was at this time that I was fascinated to discover that a family friend, who lived at Edington and needed to make regular day trips to see a specialist at a London hospital, still favoured making the journey from Edington Burtle station to Waterloo via Templecombe, rather than from Taunton or Bridgwater to Paddington.

While I was working in the Bristol divisional offices early in 1966 as part of my Railway Studentship programme I was involved briefly in the production of the emergency notices postponing the closure of the S&D because of problems with the replacement bus services. How I wish I could have been part of a cancellation of the closure, rather than mere postponement.

Even in more recent years the S&D connections keep coming along. For three years in the 1970s I helped run summer camps for teenagers at Norton Hill School at Midsomer Norton, and at that time the old station there was part of the school's facilities. I remember looking around the near-derelict premises with nostalgia, even then, and wondering if they would ever see live trains again.

A team photograph at the Bridgwater goods office taken in 1964. From left to right, David Herring, Jack Carpenter, Derek Crocker, Charlie Fuller, Bill Boyce, Jack Warren, unknown, Mr. Saunders (stationmaster), unknown, Walt Carey, Ken Creedy (rear), Graham Hughes (front) and Harold Oates.
(*David Herring collection*)

In recent years the Sainsbury's supermarket in Bridgwater has occupied most of the site of the former Bridgwater North S&D station and sidings. This is the usual place for our family shopping, and many times as I enter the store I glance at the rather dirty plaque sited on the wall near the entrance.

The family dog and I sometimes go for a walk along the footpath established on the trackbed between Bawdrip and Cossington, and it's easy to imagine that I can hear the ghosts of the old branch trains. And then, on the very day that I agreed with Alan to write these memories for his next book, I was driving on the M5 motorway near Bridgwater when I passed a low-loader carrying S&D 7F loco, number 53809. I just cannot get away from the S&D; what conclusions do I draw from my experiences of this amazing railway, which although deeply asleep, just refuses to die?

I left British Rail employment in 1967, completely disillusioned with the apparent lack of vision regarding the future of the railway infrastructure. Like many others, I very much wanted to see and be part of a modern railway, but not the wholesale slaughter of a great national asset. One couldn't justify the retention of every branch line, even, sadly, the Evercreech Junction to Highbridge section, but the rest of the S&D cried out for sensible rationalisation. Single track with passing loops would have been quite sufficient over the whole length, even from Bristol through Mangotsfield to Yate and Bath. (How useful the Yate route would be now on occasion as an alternative to the congested line to the north through Filton and Bristol Parkway.) Bath Green Park, or a nearby location, could have easily functioned as a single terminus platform with simple in and out movements, which would take very little reversing time with modern DMU stock.

Today the line would provide a very useful commuter route in both directions to and from Bath. There are rapidly growing communities at Radstock, Midsomer Norton, Shepton Mallet, Evercreech, Wincanton, Templecombe, Sturminster Newton, Blandford Forum, and other places along the old line that would benefit greatly from a through rail route. At Evercreech the New station would serve the community and the one-time Junction could now be just a plain single line without a station, while at Templecombe the lower platform on the S&D line would be sufficient with a stairs/lift connection with the upper platform. As a secondary cross country route with class 158-type trains from Bristol/South Wales, Birmingham, etc. to the South coast at Poole/Bournemouth, the whole line would surely be as useful and popular today as the parallel routes are from Bath Spa to Weymouth and Southampton. Maybe this is all just a dream, but just maybe, one day ... ?

Eric Miles is seen here in Bridgwater signalbox. He started on the S&D in 1949 at Blandford Forum as a porter, and then progressed to a signalman. Over the next 25 years he worked in nearly every signalbox on the S&D. He was a true gentleman, and people like Eric were the heart of the Somerset & Dorset. (*Connie Miles collection*)

(*above*) A turn of the century photograph of railway staff taken at Bridgwater. The young lad second from the right in the front row looks far too young to be working. (*SDRT collection*)

(*below*) Horse and cart is the order of the day as the drayman sets off from Bridgwater with his deliveries for the town and surrounding villages. It was the practice for the drayman to participate in a cup of cider when calling on outlying farms. Sometimes if the horse knew the route, he would bring the cart back to the yard while the drayman slept it off in the back. (*SDRT collection*)

(*left*) On 6 April 1959 Shapwick signalman Walter Cook exchanges tablets with fireman John Rice who is in the cab of 4F No.44417 on a Highbridge-bound train. (*Roger Joanes*)

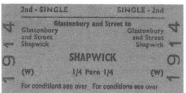

(*right*) Walter Cook is seen here in the 1950s with a member of the public at Shapwick. Walter started as a porter at Bason Bridge, later moved to Edington Junction and then became a signalman. He lived at Catcott Crossing with his wife who was the crossing keeper there. Note the wide spacing of loop lines, supposedly due to the line originally being built to broad gauge. (*Joe Moss/R.S. Carpenter collection*)

(*left*) An earlier photograph of Catcott Crossing in the 1930s when Bill Randall and his wife Emmaline lived there. Bill spent over 50 years on the S&D, starting as a porter at Masbury in 1914 and finishing as a guard at Templecombe. In this lovely shot of Emmaline's family we have, from left to right, her mother Ada Spragg, brother Sam, Emmaline who manned the crossing, and her father also named Sam. Note how near the track is to the crossing house. (*Jim Randall collection*)

(*left*) A close up of Ivatt Tank No.41249 at Ashcott station in March 1966. This was the last engine that Tony Rossiter fired on. It is seen here returning light engine back to Highbridge. (*Janet Rossiter*)

(*right*) I have a special affection for driver Ronald (Chummy) Andrews as he looks out of his cab. In the 1980s when I first started interviewing staff on the S&D, I drove from Chelmsford to Highbridge and back again in the same day to interview Chummy. My wife Christine thought I was mad. Chummy was the first person I ever interviewed and I shall always remember that day with fondness. (*Barry Andrews collection*)

(*left*) 2-6-2T class 3 No.82001 passing Ashcott sidings with the 09.45 passenger train from Highbridge to Templecombe train in 1965. Note the Standard Ten motor vehicle on the right belonging to porter Archie Atwell. (*Janet Rossiter*)

Bill Pike

My family all worked on the Somerset & Dorset Railway. My grandmother Florence worked the gates at Stone End Crossing on the Bridgwater branch; my grandfather Christopher Pike was on the permanent way on the Bridgwater branch; my father Ernest was a porter at Glastonbury; uncle Bill was a goods/passenger guard at Broadstone; and my father-in-law Reg Atyeo was a ganger.

I started as a junior porter and signal lampman at Glastonbury station in the early 1950s; part of my duties was to operate the gates at Dye House Lane Crossing. I also had to make sure all the oil lamps for the signals and station were kept alight. To go to work I would travel from Edington Junction to Glastonbury. A few times I drove the passenger train under the watchful eye of driver 'Chummy' Andrews and many a time I acted as guard on the train while the real guard Herbie Jenkins picked out his horses from the paper. Other porters there at this time were Taffy Grant, Jim Jamieson, Ted Cook, Bert Hutchings and Percy Bishop. The two foremen were Ralph Poore and Hughie Durston. Other staff I knew included goods guards Joe Hill and Ted Christopher with footplate crew Lou Moxey, Bill Parsons, Joe Prentice, Frank Salter and John Rice.

When I was on the late turn Harry Jeans, the signalman at Glastonbury, used to let me pull-push the levers while he had his cup of cocoa. One evening in 1958 I opened the gates to let the 8.00pm goods through to Evercreech. She had a maximum load on as she pulled at slow speed, puffing hard through the station, blowing red hot coals from the chimney. Going up Pylle Bank she broke a coupling and the rear end of the train ran back to West Pennard. The signalman was informed by the crossing keeper and set the line to run into a siding. It came through at high speed and hit the stop blocks and part of the train ended up in a field. The guard still stayed in his van and was later found walking towards Glastonbury in a confused state.

Later I got a job as a passenger parcels driver delivering all kinds of things from nameplates for coffins, person's ashes for undertakers and boxes of cash to be taken to banks where we put them into large safes. Once I was asked to get into the bedroom window of a lady's house; she had locked herself out and I had to open the door for her.

The railway from Glastonbury to West Pennard and Glastonbury to Wells ran together nearly to Tin Bridge. Sometimes the last trains to Wells and West Pennard pulled away together and they would have a race until the two trains went their different ways. I have also seen the 5.30pm train to Highbridge have a race with the Bridgwater train starting at Edington. The two tracks only went a short way though.

The British Railways lorry Bill Pike drove while delivering parcels and other goods around the Glastonbury area in the 1950s. The vehicle was a Morris Commercial box wagon seen here at the station on a very sunny day. (*Bill Pike*)

(*above*) An unidentified 0-6-0 Collett on duty with a two-coach passenger train for Evercreech Junction is passing the elegant 29-lever Glastonbury signalbox in the 1960s. (*Paul Strong*)

(*left*) An evocative sight when horse power was the norm for delivering goods around the villages and towns. It looks like some kinds of skins are being unloaded by the station staff at Glastonbury, maybe for Clarks Shoe Factory, c.1900s. (*SDRT collection*)

(*above*) Bathed in sunshine, and sitting on the running plate of 3F No.43356 at Glastonbury in the 1950s, are goods shed foreman Bill Milton, signalman Roy Davies and shunter Ken Atkins. (*David Milton*)

(*right*) In the cab of 1P No.1371 is fireman Maurice Cook who later became a driver on the S&D. He spent most of his working life on the branch. His brother Norman and his father Ern were also on the branch and his wife Norah worked in the booking office at Highbridge. (*Barry Andrews collection*)

0-6-0 3F No.43218 on duty with a goods train at Glastonbury. Standing next to the loco is driver Ronald Andrews and guard Frank Packer. In the cab is fireman Terry Fry. (*SDRT collection*)

(*left*) Rounding the curve at Glastonbury on 7 June 1964 is a Home Counties Railway Society Special, double headed by 7F No.53807 and 4F No.44558. We like the gentleman's headgear as he enjoys a fine view of the locos. (*Peter Morton*)

(*right*) It is always nice to have photographs of S&D railwaymen that haven't been seen before; without them there wasn't a railway. In this 1950s picture, which was taken at Glastonbury station, we have, from left to right, George Hamm who had a taxi stand at the station and drove a big Austin Princess; George Hembury who was a booking and parcels clerk; foreman Hugh Durston; and another booking and parcels clerk Stuart Pugh. (*Bill Pike*)

(*left*) The special train which celebrated the centenary of the Somerset Central Railway on 28 August 1954, seen at Glastonbury with driver Bill Peck and fireman Maurice Cook on the 3F No.43201. Note the photographer on the left, sadly with only one leg. (*Bill Pike*)

(*right*) Taken on 1 April 1949 at Polsham station is 0-4-4T No.58047 propelling a Wells to Glastonbury motor train with auto coach No.24477. (*Joe Moss/ R.S. Carpenter collection*)

(*below*) A well-known S&D character on the right at Polsham station is Stan Ford, to the left of him a young guard. Stan lived at the station house with his wife. Paul Fry, a former colleague of Stan, relates the following story.

Stan was a lorry driver at Wells Priory Road station for many years. He was a portly man and because of his weight the seat of his lorry gradually collapsed. While he was on leave, a relief driver took over his round and had a problem driving the lorry because of the seat. He went to the local scrap yard next to the goods station and found a sheet of mild steel which he put under the seat to give it a firm base. All went well for the week of Stan's holiday. Stan came back to work on the Monday, loaded up his lorry and started off up the station approach at his usual steady pace. However when Stan drove over a large pothole, the lorry gave quite a lurch and he was seen to abandon ship as fast as he could, amidst clouds of smoke and flames. What had happened was that his weight on the seat bent the sheet of mild steel down-wards and it made contact with the lorry battery terminals, producing a spectacular firework display between Stan's legs, and part of the seat caught fire. Stan was not worried about the lorry or load, only about his din-ner which was in the cab. (*Joe Moss/R. S. Carpenter collection*)

(*above*) Class 1P No.58086 takes a rest at Wells S&D shed in 1951 between working passenger trains to and from Glastonbury. (*F.A. Wycheley/Keith Barrett collection*)

(*below*) An early Daimler lorry owned by Willmotts Motor Transport of Wells with its driver. We wonder if it ever picked up goods from Priory Road railway station? (*David Sheldon collection*)

(*left*) Signalman Joe Wheeler looks happy here at Wells station. Joe was formerly a signalman at Wookey and had a pronounced Somerset accent. S&D railwayman Paul Fry recalls that when passenger trains came in Joe would stand on the platform and shout out, 'Ookey, Ookey, Ookey, ere' for the benefit of the passengers. (*Peter Hitchcock*)

(*right*) Four railwaymen, with many years service between them, enjoy having their photograph taken in September 1963 at Wells. In the picture are, from left to right, guard Jack Davies, fireman David Shepherd, carriage and wagon examiner Bert Iles and driver Harry Viles. (*Peter Hitchcock*)

(*below*) A team photograph at Wells on the last day of passenger service into Wells in September 1963. From left to right are guard Max Biggs, guard Peter Hitchcock (who was travelling back on the cushions to Bristol) and carriage and wagon examiner Bert Iles. Peter joined the S&D in 1944 as a junior porter; later he went to the parcels office and worked with horses delivering around Bath. He then became a travelling porter between Bath and Binegar. In 1951 he worked in and around Bristol as a shunter and then became a guard. When he was working with the horses he used to deliver to Colmer's at Bath. One of the shop assistants always came out to give the horse a sugar lump. One day when the horse was waiting for his sugar lump, this person didn't turn up as he was on holiday, so the horse decided to go through the shop window and fetch it himself. (*Peter Hitchcock*)

Michael Eavis, CBE

I had the pleasure of meeting Michael Eavis at his home at Worthy Farm, which is situated between Pylle and West Pennard. He is the founder of the world famous Glastonbury Music Festival which is held on his farm each June. He received his CBE for his services to music. The trackbed of the old Somerset & Dorset Railway ran across his land, which has been in his family for generations.

* * *

My first recollection of travelling on the Somerset & Dorset Railway was in the late 1940s. I went by train from West Pennard station on our chapel's Sunday School outing to Burnham-on-Sea. There was great excitement as we boarded the train. We travelled across the Moors through Glastonbury, Ashcott, Shapwick and Edington, where we could see the cranes flying up into the sky as our train passed them. We saw their nests in the trees all the way through to Burtle. On reaching Burnham we all had a great day out.

When we were younger my friend Jasser Perry and I would put pennies on the line near Steanbow Crossing. It was a huge excitement to see the pennies flattened by the trains. My brothers Patrick, Peter, Philip and sister Susan would also go down to the line and watch the trains go by. On Worthy Farm there was a walk through to take the cattle across the railway line from one side of the farm to the other. We called this field 'Halts' as the trains would sometimes be halted to allow us to take the cattle across the line. There were gates there which we used to operate ourselves. Later we would bring the cattle back for milking. We used to set the milking time by the train going past at 7.40am. If we hadn't started milking the cows by the time the train went by we were late for the milk lorry. Our milk went by tanker to Evercreech.

I remember in 1958 when the afternoon milk train from Highbridge to Templecombe ran away and smashed into the buffers at West Pennard station (Alan's book *Celebration of the Somerset & Dorset Railway* has the full story of the incident, by fireman Roy Hix, who was on the train's engine). When it passed our farm we saw the wagons going backwards and the engine going forward. The coupling had snapped as the train headed up the steep embankment at Pylle Bank. I quickly made my way to West Pennard station in my Morris Minor pick-up truck to see what was going to happen. Other farmers had also arrived.

On reaching the station, there were wagons lying on their sides after they had hit the buffers at speed. There was liquid milk, tins of milk and large rolls of barbed wire all mixed up in heaps. The West Pennard signalman Tom Salisbury who was in charge of the box at the time had carried out the right procedure in making sure the run-away wagons went into the goods siding.

Looking at all the rolls of barbed wire I could see a use for them as could the other farmers who were there. Tom didn't seem to have a problem in us helping ourselves to the wire which was a very expensive item. We all had about 20 rolls each and I took mine back to the farm. The wire was heavily barbed and was being delivered to sites where they were putting up pylons. The wire was being placed around the pylons to stop people climbing up them. We put the wire all around the fields but unfortunately there was a downside to all of this. The wire was heavily barbed as mentioned and very sharp. When the cattle hopped over the fence they got ripped to pieces and it also cut their udders so it was the worst thing we could have done to take that wire. We took the wire down immediately. There is a moral there, don't take anything that doesn't belong to you.

None of our animals as far as I can remember strayed on to the railway line. The fences were well made and even today, 50 years on, they are still as strong as ever.

When I was a teenager I used to travel by train from West Pennard to Burnham for various events and of course do a bit of courting with a number of girls. The social life there was very good and I had a great time. I don't know why but the girls from Burnham always seemed to be far prettier. I went to London by train quite a few times, going from West Pennard to Evercreech then on to Templecombe and then to London.

I well remember the crossing at Cockmill. They had their water delivered there by train daily as there was no mains water. The crossing was run by Mrs Higgins who was a strong lady and certainly told the footplate crews if she wasn't happy about getting her water on time, or maybe they hadn't dropped off enough coal for her. Her husband was partial to a drop of scrumpy and would disappear to *The Bush* Public House which wasn't far from our farm. It was built for the railway workers when they were laying the track back in the mid 1800s; it is no longer there. After his quota of cider Mr. Higgins would stagger back to the crossing house or if Mrs Higgins wasn't in a good mood he would sleep under the stars somewhere.

I knew Charlie King, one of the S&D drivers. Charlie went to a chapel in Burnham-on-Sea where I got married to Ruth. Before we got married Ruth would come and stay for the weekend with me at the farm. On the Monday I would take her to West Pennard station to catch the 7.40am school train so she could get back to work. When Charlie was driving this train he would always look out for us on the bridge. On one occasion we were running late and the train had just moved off. Charlie saw my green pick-up coming over the bridge. He stopped the train which had moved on about 200 yards and then reversed the train back to the platform to pick up Ruth. Charlie always said that if he could help his customers he would.

When speaking to Alan we put on our rose tinted glasses and thought, if the S&D was running now, I could bring in 180,000 people and maybe some of the bands to the Glastonbury Music Festival, direct to the site by train. We could call the station Worthy Farm Halt situated between Pylle and West Pennard. Wouldn't that be fantastic! When Beeching carried out his cuts to the railways in the 1960s, he and many others hadn't anticipated what a devastating effect it had on our communities. When the S&D closed we bought the trackbed that went through our farm from the railway authorities, which was about a quarter of a mile in length. Today the trackbed is used as the main exit for the Festival, so the old S&D is still being used for customers. I would like to wish Alan and Christine all the best with this new excellent book on the old Somerset & Dorset Railway.

* * *

As I left Worthy Farm I, of course, thanked Michael Eavis for allowing me into his home to record his memories. In our conversation we also spoke about music and I mentioned that I had played in a band, *Quota Plus*, in London in the 1970s (*I am second from the left in this photo*). I also mentioned that he was probably trying to organise bands now for the 2009 Glastonbury Music Festival. With a glint in his eye he said to me: 'Are you going to reform your band to play Glastonbury for me?' After getting over the initial shock I said 'I wish'. Or did he really mean it?

(*above*) A view of the station buildings at West Pennard. On the right is the old tariff shed and the main building housing the booking office, waiting room and the staff quarters. On the left is the 23-lever signalbox. What a lovely view that must have given the signalman when he was enjoying his morning cuppa on a bright spring day. (*Keith Barrett collection*)

(*left*) An Evercreech Junction passenger train for Highbridge entering West Pennard station with motive power 3F No.43436 in charge. (*R.E. Toop*)

(*right*) Ivatt LMS 2MT No.41214 engulfed in smoke and steam is just about to go under West Pennard overbridge (No.257) with a local for Evercreech Junction in January 1965.
(*Paul Strong*)

(*left*) On a misty day over the levels in October 1964 Collett No.2218 steams towards West Pennard with an up freight.
(*Paul Strong*)

(*right*) Workmates together on the footplate of 3F No.3194 are fireman Alan Jones on the left and driver Ronald Andrews, c.1940s.
(*Barry Andrews collection*)

A photograph that soaks up the atmosphere of the S&D, as 3F No.43682 hauls a passenger train through Pylle with a Highbridge bound train. (*R.E. Toop*)

(*above*) This wonderful postcard of Elbow Corner Crossing was sent to a family member by Walter Griffin, one of the sons of crossing keepers Jane and her husband John in 1906. In the picture Jane is on the right with John next to her; the gentleman on the left is unknown. Walter worked on the S&D with his brothers Frank, a signalman at Bath Junction, and Fred, a signalman at Midsomer Norton. Another brother Alfred was a goods guard at Bath Green Park. This certainly was an S&D family affair. (*Brenda Griffin collection*)

(*right*) 4F No.44422 draws in to Pylle Halt in 1958 with an excursion train for Bournemouth. The Highbridge driver looking out of the cab is Bill May who spent his whole working life on the S&D. (*Peter Pike*)

(*left*) Working towards home are a pair of Ivatt 2-6-2Ts headed by No.41307 and No.41249 on 5 March 1966 near Pylle Bank on a LCGB Somerset & Dorset Rail Tour. (*Maurice Cook collection*)

(*below*) Grace Lintern in her Morris Commercial at Bruton Road Crossing in the 1930s. (*Max Shore collection*)

(right) A lovely photograph of Bruton Road Crossing keeper Ellen (Nellie) Lintern, taken in the 1930s. (*Max Shore collection*)

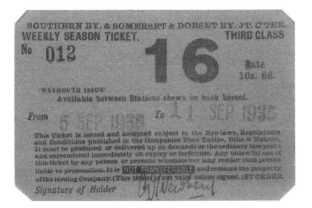

(below) A family gathering at Bruton Road Crossing in the 1930s. From left to right, back row, George Lintern and his father William Lintern; centre row, Dolly Lintern, Ellen Lintern, Grace Lintern; and in the front row are Bill Lintern and Grace Lintern junior. (*Max Shore collection*)

The landscape is briefly disturbed at Cole as Standard class 5 No.73047 makes a fine sight with a Leicester to Bournemouth express in 1956. (*Paul Strong*)

Class 2P No.40700 makes steady progress as it coasts around Cole curve ahead of the 13.10 Bath to Templecombe stopping train. (*SDRT collection*)

A splendid panoramic view on a crisp autumn day in 1964, as a Collett is seen in the distance coasting with a moderate load at Pitcombe just south of Cole. (*Paul Strong*)

Tony Christie

We met singer Tony Christie on the high seas. Tony was the largest selling act in 2005/6 in the UK. His record *Is This The Way To Amarillo* sold well over one million copies as did his album *The Definitive Collection*. Chatting to him we got on to the topic of railways, as one does. Tony like me was an ardent trainspotter when we were both much younger, and with this in mind, he very kindly agreed to write his memories of those days.

* * *

What is it that makes men of a certain age (usually middle and beyond) go doey eyed at the thought of a Pink Floyd, Deep Purple, or Led Zeppelin revival? It's the same sort of thing that happens to railway enthusiasts whenever the word 'Steam' is mentioned. It's all about nostalgia. (Who said nostalgia's not what it used to be?)

As a small boy growing up in South Yorkshire just after the war, steam locomotion was as normal to me as, say, computer games seem to be to today's young kids. It all started when I was about ten years old. My grandfather used to take me fishing. This involved a train journey from Conisbrough, where I lived, to Keadby in Lincolnshire. The Stainforth and Keadby canal in those days was particularly good for coarse fishing. On the way, there was a stop of about ten minutes at Doncaster station. It was

there that I saw my first 'Streak', sitting on the adjacent line. It was love at first sight. I have to point out that a 'Streak' was our local nickname for the A4 series, probably because of its shape. There it was, not a machine, but a living, breathing, beautiful beast. I was hooked. From that moment on I became a trainspotter. It became an obsession with me. I would spend all my summer holidays sitting on either Doncaster or Sheffield station, armed only with a packet of sandwiches, a bottle of water and most importantly, my copy of Ian Allan's *Combined Volume of British Railways Locomotives.*

Doncaster station became my second home because it was on the main line between London and Scotland's East coast. The amount of traffic in those days was very high, an absolute trainspotters' paradise. There was a

camaraderie with the other enthusiasts. It was almost like the bush telegraph. Whenever a London to Edinburgh train was due either to go through, or better still, stop at Doncaster, there was a kind of expectant excitement that you could feel in the atmosphere, and almost every time we were not disappointed. There would be a 'Streak' for us to 'cop' (underline in our spotter's books) or the almost as beautiful 'Winnies' or Windshielders (A3s). Sometimes, but not very often, there would be a loco from another region, like the Britannia Class which again we had our own name for, in this case Robin Hood class after one of the 'namers' in that category.

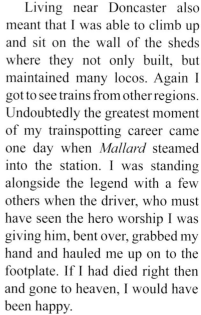

Living near Doncaster also meant that I was able to climb up and sit on the wall of the sheds where they not only built, but maintained many locos. Again I got to see trains from other regions. Undoubtedly the greatest moment of my trainspotting career came one day when *Mallard* steamed into the station. I was standing alongside the legend with a few others when the driver, who must have seen the hero worship I was giving him, bent over, grabbed my hand and hauled me up on to the footplate. If I had died right then and gone to heaven, I would have been happy.

It's a strange thing about railway enthusiasts, but it's almost like belonging to an exclusive club. We seem to be drawn to one another. Even the guy who ran my fan club for years, Ray Smyth, I found out much later was a fanatic. Two years ago I went to Nashville to make an album with a record producer called Graeme Pleeth. While all the musicians sat around talking crochets, we sat around discussing which different railway exhibitions there were to see.

Being asked by Alan and Christine to write my memories for their book has been most therapeutic for me. It has brought back into my mind a period of my life which, when I now think back, was very rich, not in monetary terms, but I consider myself lucky to have witnessed the truly Great Age of the Railways. You can't buy memories.

The Bath Extension – Evercreech Junction to Bath

John Simms

In 1874 the Somerset and Dorset Railway had been leading an independent existence for 12 years, running small trains behind small engines through market towns and villages between the Bristol Channel at Highbridge and the English Channel at Poole. Business was little more than adequate and the concern was sliding gently into insolvency and a probable takeover by a larger company. But the S&D was never less than perverse and instead of 'going quietly' it embarked on an expansion, driving a line from Evercreech, up and over the Mendip Hills and into Bath where it would join the Midland Railway and share Green Park station. Along the way the new line would gain mineral traffic from the coalfield around Radstock and Midsomer Norton and also various quarries.

Against logical expectations the new railway was indeed built. Unfortunately it was done on the cheap and saddled the S&DR with a baleful legacy. Murderously hard climbs up the Mendip slopes, tight curves as the line sought the easiest route (including part of the old Somersetshire Coal Canal Tramway), too many miles of single-line track, inadequate engines – both in terms of numbers and power – and a staff who were badly or barely trained, working impossibly long hours for pay that was almost derisory. Inevitably matters ended in bankruptcy and in 1876 the Midland Railway and the London and South Western moved in rapidly, whilst the Great Western was biding its time, and took over. And so was born the Somerset and Dorset Joint Railway.

Both the Midland and the LSWR were excellent railways amongst the Victorian companies but before they could do much with their new property the chickens of the old company came home to a vengeful roosting. On the evening of 7 August 1876 there was a major accident at Foxcote near Radstock involving an excursion train carrying crowds home from Bath Regatta and 12 passengers were killed. The Board of Trade's Official Enquiry found a shambolic state of affairs including a boy signalman on duty who was not strong enough to pull his signal levers and the subsequent report was damning. But under the new regime matters began to change. The Midland supplied adequate locomotives, the South Western took the track in hand and improvements came rapidly.

Even so some matters could not be altered. One of the worst was Combe Down Tunnel which faced trains slogging up the steep climb from and to Bath. It was long, the engines' chimneys were within an inch or so of the top of the tunnel and there were no ventilating shafts. Somerset and Dorset enginemen going about their daily work were confronted with a vision of hell that a medieval preacher would have recognized, in a stifling hole of utter darkness with their locomotive's smoke beating into the cabs. Nor could the gradients be eased. S&D crews 'rated' the types of engine they came to work freight trains with, not just on their ability to pull trains but also on their braking capacity.

The wayside stations were neat and tidy buildings of stone and a typical example is being lovingly restored at Midsomer Norton. As with the rest of the S&D the staff who manned these and ran the trains all knew each other and their regular passengers, and were welcoming to strangers. The scenery was often spectacular but the gradients and curves meant that passengers had a good long time to view it.

However if any railway line could be described as having a split personality it was the Bath Extension. For much of the year it was a country railway with heavy mineral traffic at its north end and stopping passenger trains wending their way along. Once a day came the Manchester to Bournemouth through train, the 'Pines Express', always the pride of the line. But as holiday traffic to the South Coast was developed by the MR and the LSWR, and their successors the LMS and Southern Railways, for some Saturdays in the summer months holiday passenger trains came to flood the line's capacity. By the British Railways era of the 1950s, summer Saturdays saw virtually every engine that could turn a wheel pounding the lines of coaches up to Masbury Summit and then dropping down off the Mendips. Single-line sections of track were never unoccupied, signalmen worked flat out throughout their shifts and locomen tried to persuade heavy freight engines to run passenger trains to time.

And all of this was recorded for posterity by a photographer of the highest talent. Ivo Peters was never a railwayman but he was respected by the crews of the Somerset and Dorset for the brilliance with which he recorded their efforts and shared the pictures with them, unfailingly polite and a gentleman to all. A one-time racing driver his Sports Bentley saloon car was deployed to allow him to move from location to location. In this way he could take several photographs of unusual train workings at various locations. But unwittingly he also highlighted the fatal weakness of the Somerset and Dorset. No matter how good the driver and how powerful the car the fact that round rural Somerset roads he could stay ahead of the train reflected how slowly even the best trains were moving. Passengers en route to or from the South Coast had a journey that tested their patience, particularly when the day was hot and the train full, and as the private car became affordable the short-lived boom in passenger figures fell away.

By 1962 the Western Region of British Railways was managing the line and had enough spare capacity on their route via Oxford and Basingstoke to the South Coast to divert the trains away from that long and un-economic slog over the Mendips. In 1963, for the first time in its history, the Bath Extension was a dormant rural line with only local slow trains and a declining volume of freight making its way through stations whose paintwork was faded and which began to look in need of care, no matter how hard the still-loyal staff battled.

The closure proposal, though not unexpected, still came as a shock. It was bitterly fought with conscientious railwaymen, who in the hard winter of 1962/63 had risked their lives to keep the line open, staging public protests. They were backed by local communities such as Wellow which feared isolation if the railway went and with it the dedication of the men and women workers. The line had been known, with some exasperated affection as the 'Slow and Dirty'. The staff who had replied 'Serene and Delightful' now spoke of 'Sabotaged and Defeated' and even the final act went on for a shabby three months after the closure was postponed from 31 December 1965.

The family atmosphere of the Somerset and Dorset was as evident on the scarp slopes of the Mendips as elsewhere. In the Second World War female station staff came from families such as my own where fathers and brothers were already on the line and marriages followed with receptions held in the *Railway Arms* or *The Station Inn*. Flowers were tended in station gardens and woe betide the fireman caught helping himself to a marrow from the vegetable patch behind the signalbox. He and his driver might find themselves subject to a little more delay next time they were heading for home at the end of their shift. And perhaps the true voice of the rural railwayman, not just that of the Somerset and Dorset, was the cry of a 'bobby' heard coming up from a station platform into his signalbox as a travelling pet tried to escape: 'Stop that dog, he's a parcel!'

A marvellous photograph of Evercreech Junction signalman William Copp with all his family, c.1910. From left to right are William Copp, his wife Caroline, his son William Stanley, daughters Constance Kate and Beatrice May, John Copp (Williams's father) and daughter Mabel. The photo was taken outside their cottage, aptly named Copp's Cottage, Southwood, Evercreech, which is still there today. It is interesting to note that when William was at Evercreech in 1885 he was earning 20/- per week as a signalman. (*Rita Pettet collection*)

(*above*) Fireman Mike Lewis watches the cameraman as the branch train rejoins the main line at Evercreech Junction North with Collett No.2218 at the head of the train. (*Paul Strong*)

(*below*) This 1931 picture is one of those classic Evercreech Junction photographs, as 4-4-0 No.635 with a Bournemouth train takes on water, as one of the crew manoeuvres the wheel. To the left of him a gang of permanent way men are having a yarn, probably about how many pints they are going to enjoy at the *Railway Hotel* later, which was next to the Junction. (*Richard Dagger collection*)

John Simms

Evercreech Junction always seemed to be something of a frontier post. To the north the branch line to Burnham went straight ahead whilst the main line swung away as trains began the slog over the Mendips to Shepton Mallet, Masbury, Radstock and Bath. There were the freight yards at the north end and the siding in the station area itself was used either to stable the branch line train for Burnham or, on Summer Saturdays, the line of steam engines waiting to assist the passenger trains over the 1 in 50 climb towards the Midlands and the North of England. Looking southwards the line crossed the road on a level crossing under the watchful eye of the signalman in the tall South box. For passengers the view through the window changed again from the high limestone country of the Mendips or the flatlands and drainage ditches of the Somerset Levels to rich, rolling agricultural land, more in line with what the general public thought of as West of England scenery. Outside, the flavour of the accents of the railway staff began to subtly change as the trains passed from Somerset into Dorset. On the through services from the north heading for Bournemouth the speed of the train became more rapid.

(*left*) A stalwart of the Somerset & Dorset Railway was foreman Vic Freak seen here at Evercreech Junction. Look at those fire buckets, freshly painted and all in a straight line. (*Vic Freak collection*)

(*right*) It is Christmas Eve at Evercreech Junction station with stationmaster Alec Stowe in the middle of the photograph leading the carol singing, c.1950s. To the left, holding a shunting pole with a lamp attached to it, is Highbridge passenger guard Arthur Blackborow. Behind Alec Stowe is signal lampman Vic Freak and to the right with only their heads showing are Zoë Stowe and goods guard Joe Hill. Holding the other shunting pole is station foreman Mark Lambert. (*John Eaton*)

(*above*) The *Railway Hotel* seen here at Evercreech was a favourite for the staff on the S&D. It was well-known up and down the line for serving a great pint of beer. In front of the public house is William Jewell who was the landlord for many years and in the doorway is his wife. Their daughter Mary Jewell (*right*) took over the running of the Railway Hotel when her parents retired. Mary later married a former fireman on the S&D, Les Haines. The bar looks immaculate and the Double Diamond sign on the right of Mary reminds me of my first pint at the *Spencer's Arms* in Hornchurch, Essex. I must have liked the beer so much that I went and played football for Romford Brewery who distributed the beer. (*both photographs Mary Haines collection*)

(*left*) As the crew take on water the driver, Art Hatcher, lights the lamps of class 4 No.76027 ready to work a down service from Evercreech Junction. (*Roger Holmes/ Hugh Davies collection*)

(*right*) Having worked from Bournemouth Central, 7F No.53807 and 4F No.44558 arrives at Evercreech Junction with the northbound Home Counties Railway Society S&D Rail Tour on 7 June 1964. The crews on the 7F were driver Alwyn Hannam and fireman Don Garrett and on the 4F were driver Fred Fisher and fireman Bruce Briant. (*Alan Mitchard*)

(*left*) Ivatt class 2 No.41242 takes a rest at Evercreech Junction before it takes a train to Highbridge, c.1964. The crew on the platform are fireman Terry Fry and driver Dennis Nettley. (*R.K. Blencowe collection*)

(*left*) With plenty of steam on show LMS Stanier class 5 No.44826 is topped up with water at Evercreech Junction by the fireman for the trip to Bournemouth, whilst the driver, Albert Good, operates the wheel. (*Keith Barrett collection*)

(*below*) Driver Tom Gunning on the footplate of 2P No.40700 with his good friend Norman Gibbons, who was the driver on the other assisting engine in the middle road at Evercreech Junction. (*Pauline Keen collection*)

(*above*) Standard class 4 Tank No.80134 stops at an immaculate Evercreech New station, before making a brisk getaway with a northbound local service. (*Keith Barrett collection*)

(*below*) A deserted Evercreech New station except for the signalman on the right, as a Bath-bound stopper with Standard 4 No.76027 approaches. (*Keith Barrett collection*)

John Eaton

Following my memories of the Somerset & Dorset which appeared in Alan's last book, *Celebration of the Somerset & Dorset Railway*, I recall three other incidents.

One day during the summer of 1955, when I was on porter's duty at Evercreech New station on the late turn, there was a terrific thunder storm. I was standing in the booking office doorway when a thunderbolt hit the station and I was blown right back into the booking office. At the same time the signalbox was struck by lightning which blew out the telephones and burnt out some of the instruments. The signalman, Ted Lambert, ran out of the signalbox in terror. I rushed to inform the stationmaster Reg Jeans at his home nearby and also the signalman Sid Pitt who was scheduled to relieve Ted at 2.30am.

When I got back to the station, Bath control was on the GPO telephone asking Ted what had happened. Engineers got the rail telephones working temporarily and all the instruments were repaired next day by the signal and telegraph department. Ted certainly had a lucky escape that night. His sister is the well-known Betty Spiller who was a porteress at Evercreech Junction in the 1940s.

On another occasion I was in Evercreech New signalbox receiving training from signalman Ted Lambert. Ted told me that all the signals were in the off position for the 1.10pm Bournemouth West to Bristol Temple Meads train. Ted was looking out of the signalbox window when the guard shouted out: 'Why is the starting signal at danger?' On investigation, Ted and the guard found that the bolt connecting the signal arm rod was broken. Ted told the guard it was all right to proceed while Ted and the stationmaster, Reg Jeans, found some rope and fixed the rod temporarily until it was repaired the next day.

The Somerset and Dorset Railway had its fair share of personalities; one of them was Evercreech Junction signalman Les Williams (*pictured below*). One day I was visiting Templecombe No.2 signalbox and signalman Harry Steel told me this story. He and his wife met up with Les and his wife one evening at the *Railway Hotel* in Templecombe. Les and his good lady were already there and enjoying a drink. Harry asked them what they would like to drink. Les replied: 'If it's okay, Harry, I would like a nice drop from the top shelf [i.e. gin] for me and the wife'. Harry said Les liked his drop of gin when anybody offered to buy him a drink; it went well with his pint of cider, he said.

Signalman Les Williams seen here in the Evercreech Junction South signalbox in the 1950s. Note the numbers above the door; I understand this was when the box was last painted. (*John Eaton*)

(*above*) A raw winter's day in January 1965, as the sun casts a shadow over Standard 4 Tank No.80081 passing the goods shed at Shepton Mallet with an up local. (*Paul Strong*)

(*below*) After re-marshalling its train, 7F No.53801 sets out to leave Shepton Mallet with a freight train for Bath in 1955. (*Keith Barrett collection*)

(*above*) This photograph is nearly 100 years old. It shows S&D drayman William (Bill) Lintern holding a young baby in front of his horse and cart at Garston Street, Shepton Mallet. (*Max Shore collection*)

(*above*) Another photograph of William Lintern in his garden playing air guitar on his fork in the 1920s. If you look to the left you can see Shepton Mallet Viaduct. (*Max Shore collection*)

(*below*) A hive of activity at Shepton Mallet as Standard 5 No.73054 takes on water whilst working a down (1X06) Bank Holiday Special excursion in 1965. (*Peter Morton*)

Brian Davis

I am now over 60 years of age and probably like all of us relate to what we did when we were younger. In my era, when growing up, it was trainspotting. I can remember it like it was yesterday, and it must have left a lasting impression on me, as now I am a very keen railway modeller, especially of the S&D. I cannot, however, remember quite how old I was when I started trainspotting but I was probably about 10 or 11. My actual interest in trains started a while before that when I was given a Triang set for Christmas. It was the usual black *Princess Elizabeth* with two short maroon coaches, an oval track and a battery controller that went from flat out to stop at the flick of a lever.

One of my earliest memories of the real thing was at Templecombe one summer in the 1950s. I well remember Merchant Navy class No.35003 *Royal Mail* flying through on an Exeter-bound train, all clean, green, noisy, smoky and still with its casing on.

I suppose that occasion with 35003 was a couple of years before I started noting the numbers. I seem to recall not being able to afford 10/6d for a combined volume so I made my own version of it from individual 2/6d regional versions, which I collected over a period of time. I still have the book, all dog-eared and rather fragile and completely priceless to me.

I have very fond memories of my visits during school holidays to see my nan at Shepton Mallet on the old Somerset & Dorset Railway. These visits were normally made during the school holidays in August between 1955 and 1963. Having lived in Surrey all my life, I was, of course, very familiar with Southern engines. It came as a bit of a shock upon my arrival at Templecombe to be hauled up to Shepton Mallet by locos of Midland origin so close to the Dorset border, especially as one of the first ones was a 4F. A freight loco on a passenger train – what next?

I didn't realise the fascination of the S&D in certain circles of the railway fraternity. If only I could have afforded a camera or even thought to have recorded the names of the many crews who allowed me up into their cabs at Shepton Mallet, Evercreech and Templecombe. I was too young and too excited to think of such things at the time. When the crews realised, from my accent, that I was from up London way, they seemed keen to know what I was doing in their neck of the woods. At that time I was quite shy and didn't say an awful lot but they were all really nice people. I couldn't always catch what they were saying with their West Country accents, especially if the engine was blowing off at the time. My mother was equally fascinated by the local lingo and would let the window down at stations just to listen to them.

I well remember on occasions being allowed up into the cabs of locos which were off the platform end at Shepton. I found it rather difficult climbing up from ground level as I hadn't mastered the art of pulling myself up using the handrails. I had to climb up the rather grubby steps and generally felt as though I would slip off. Getting back down by climbing was virtually impossible as it was like getting stuck up a tree, so I had to jump. Goodness knows what the crew thought.

One day in 1959 I made my way to Shepton Mallet station to do a bit of spotting as usual and there in the station was Standard 5 No.73028 at the head of a works train. The gang were there to re-ballast the down line and put down new sleepers as well. It must have been about 8.00am and they were on the down line about to go forward and reverse back onto the up line to start work. The crew let me up into the cab, as a lot did; they were generally quite friendly down there. We chatted for a while and the fireman gave me his knitted cloth, which I still have in a drawer at home.

Shortly afterwards, another crew arrived to take over the duty and the first crewman asked the new ones if I could stay on board. I was highly delighted when they answered yes. You can imagine my absolute joy when the driver invited me to open the regulator, which I only just managed. When the time came to stop, I just didn't have the strength to push it back again and the driver had to regain control. The train had to go forward into the sidings every now and again to let the service trains pass and then reverse back out into the platform. About midday I had to go back to my nan's for lunch, but upon my return the crew allowed me back up on the footplate again. Late in the afternoon the fireman kindly gave me a piece of his cherry cake. I stayed in the cab until tea-time.

Another time at Templecombe I got in the cab of an Armstrong on what was probably a Bath train and having had the usual chat with the crew it went quiet as they prepared for the off. They forgot I was there and started to move the train. The driver looked quite concerned and said something like: 'God, I forgot you were still here'. I replied: 'Don't worry' and I jumped off onto the platform and waved goodbye to them. Judging by the looks on their faces I think they were greatly relieved that I was none the worse for my rapid exit.

A year or two later I wandered on to the station as usual, stood in the booking hall and thought to myself, shall I have a day out somewhere. I had no idea of the distance but I decided to buy a return ticket to Exeter. It is about 80 miles from Shepton Mallet, the fare was 15/-, and I didn't even think to tell my family where I was going.

The highlight of the day occurred when I returned to Templecombe at about 9.00pm to catch the train back to Shepton Mallet. Standing in platform 3 was class 4 2-6-0 No.76019 at the head of the train. I chatted to the fireman for a while and he invited me to come up into the cab whereupon I was greeted in the usual fashion by the driver. After a couple of minutes he asked me if I had ever had a ride in an engine before, to which I replied: 'Only up and down the yard, sir.' He said: 'Where are you going?' I answered: 'Shepton Mallet' and he replied: 'Okay then, you can come in the cab with us. But keep your head down at the stations or I'll get the sack'. The fireman took my satchel and put it away for me and sat me in his seat for the whole trip. It was very dark and quite noisy, but what a thrill for a 14-year-old spotter.

As mentioned briefly in the tale about 76019, my first cab ride was on an S15 carrying out some shunting in the upper yard at Templecombe. Once

again, if my memory serves me correctly the driver actually invited me up onto the footplate and chatted while he worked. After speaking to Alan Hammond recently, crews who were friendly to us spotters in that era could have been the likes of Templecombe crews Alan Hix, Robin Gould, Tony Axford, Derek Howcutt, Ben Dyer, Richard Rendle and George Welch. The Bath crews could have been the likes of John Sawyer, Ian Bunnett, Ron Gray, Cliff Smith, Bill Rawles and Howard Reynolds; I wonder if any of them were the crews I met?

On weekdays I don't recall too many trains either calling at or passing through Shepton, but in those far off days I was quite happy just to sit in the sunshine occasionally talking to a porter whilst waiting for the next train to arrive. However the summer weekends were somewhat different. For a start I was never alone on a Saturday as I was always joined by the local spotters. We observed and noted not just the stoppers but the many expresses as well. I wonder if any of those lads might remember me, the one with the South London accent?

It would also be interesting to know if any of them actually joined the S&D. When I was very young, like a lot of young lads, I wanted to be an engine driver but by the time I was 15½ and about to leave school, I realised that working on the railways was not for me. Firstly, I didn't fancy shift work and secondly in 1963 I realised that steam was on its way out. No way would I work with diesels! Also at that time most of us lads only saw the romantic side of the railways. We didn't know about all the training, the promotion ladder or the fact that life on the footplate could be very unpleasant at times – being cold in winter and hot in summer. I do remember, however, seeing the crew of an Armstrong hauling my train from Templecombe to Shepton Mallet actually hanging on to the handrails outside the engine to escape the heat.

Just to prove a point as to how pleasant the enginemen were, in the four or five summer holidays I spent at Shepton, I got into at least 34 cabs there and at Templecombe and Evercreech but, of course, some of the cabs at Templecombe were probably on the Southern Region main line. Out of the 34, seven were 7Fs.

After 1963 my family didn't always go to Shepton Mallet for our holidays and I never saw the S&D at work again.

A vintage view taken from the footbridge on a crisp January day in 1965, as an unidentified Standard class 4 Tank prepares to stop at Shepton Mallet (Charlton Road) station on a down service. (*Paul Strong*)

Making a magnificent sight is LMS 4-4-0 2P No.630 nearing the top of Masbury Summit with a train bound for Bath. (*Keith Barrett collection*)

(*above*) Hauling their train up towards Masbury Summit on 31 July 1954 are LMS 4F No.44102 and a West Country class No.34094 *Mortehoe*. (*E.W. Fry/R.K. Blencowe collection*)

(*below*) This photograph soaks up the atmosphere of the Somerset & Dorset Railway, here at Masbury station, as pilot engine 2P No.40563 coupled together with Standard 5 No.73050 heads towards Bath. (*Norman Simmons/Hugh Davies collection*)

(*above*) I met the late Mike Fox a few times and his superb photographs of the S&D are second to none. This 2-6-4T class 4 No.80037 in the snow near Masbury sums up the quality of his work. (*Mike Fox*)

(*left*) Working hard on a down freight nearing Masbury Summit is class 7F No.53807 (with a large boiler) and banking in the rear is a Jinty from Rad-stock shed. (*Keith Barrett collection*)

(*right*) Looking in pristine condition on a bright winter's day in February 1936 is 2P No.697 with a down express near Burnt House Bridge (No.57) near Moorewood. (*Keith Barrett collection*)

(*left*) A morning departure for Standard Tank 4 No.80067 leaving Binegar with its three-coach train bound for Evercreech. The signal-box is on the up side and the main station buildings on the down side. (*E.T. Gill/R.K. Blencowe collection*)

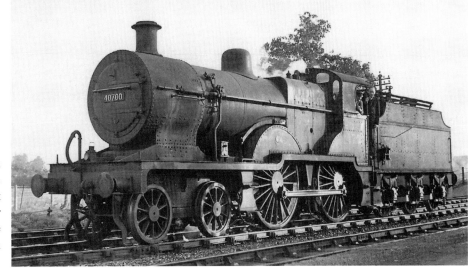

(*right*) It is a lovely summer's evening, with the late sun shining brightly on 2P No.40700 at Binegar. Bath Green Park driver Bert Reed is seen on the left in the cab with stationmaster Norman Down. (*Rita Smart collection*)

Ken Padfield

My first contact with the S&D was in 1936 when, at the age of five, and on the death of my father, my mother and I moved from Bristol to Gurney Slade to live with her parents. Their cottage was only about 300 yards from the railway between Moorewood and Binegar. My grandfather rented a large railway allotment at the foot of the embankment.

I was always aware of trains, even if, in those early days, I was not taking as much notice as I later wished I had. At that time, I also had an uncle Edgar Colbourn who was in the Radstock permanent way gang and later became a ganger. On leaving school his son, Albert, joined the S&D as a clerk at Midsomer Norton.

I attended Binegar School until the age of 11, and as the school was the other side of the railway, I passed under it four times a day going to and from school. The school itself was also within sight and sound of Binegar station. On my way to and from school I always stopped and climbed a convenient field gate and was fascinated by the down freights that were banked by a Jinty. I recall the arrival of the Black Fives with their distinctive whistles and the West Countrys and their three-cylinder exhaust beat. During the war special trains were quite frequent with many of them passing through during the hours of darkness. I do remember some of the daylight specials were hospital trains, headed by 'foreign' engines. I also think there were one or two 4-4-0s with Southern numbers.

At the age of 11 I had to move on to senior school at Shepton Mallet. This was in Whitstone Road and only a hundred yards or so from the S&D Waterloo Viaduct which partially collapsed in 1946. After a period of about a year or so my mother decided that I would be better served by receiving an education which was of a much more clerical nature. Con-sequently, in 1943, I was enrolled at Cannings College in Bath necessitating a daily journey by train between Binegar and Bath, Queen Square, as it was then known. As this period fell during the 1939-45 war, travel between Binegar and Bath was not always punctual and the carriages were anything but well-lit due to the black-out regulations. We were often an hour or so late leaving Bath in the afternoon as the train (I think it may have been the Pines or its equivalent) had been delayed in its journey south to Bath. The motive power at this time was usually LMS 2P 4-4-0 Nos.509, 696, 697, 700 and others. It was during this period that Norman Down came to Binegar to replace Jim Payne as stationmaster. I seem to remember being impressed by his height, erect bearing, officialness, his brand new uniform and shiny black boots.

As I neared my 15th birthday my mother decided that it was about time for me to start helping support her instead of her supporting me. At that time I was very friendly with David and Brian Gill. Their father, Dick, was, I think, manager of Read's Quarry at Binegar, later to become part of Roads Reconstruction (1934) Limited. He asked me what I would like to do when I left school and I assume I must have mentioned the railway because he said he would speak to Norman Down on my behalf. This he did, informing me that it was now up to me to follow up the word he had put in for me.

On approaching Norman Down (with some trepidation), I found him to be very helpful, not only obtaining the necessary form, but also helping me to complete it. In due course I was summoned to attend an examination in Bath, held, if my memory serves me correctly, in the first class waiting room at Queen Square station. This was fairly straightforward, comprising a mix of English, Maths and Geography. I also had to pass a medical examination at Bristol, which included sorting various lengths of coloured wool to ensure that I was not colour blind. I left college on Friday 26 July 1946, and duly presented myself at 8.00am on the following Monday at Binegar station.

I was welcomed by Norman Down with a chat, a list of my duties, my hours of attendance, his expectations of me and an explanation of how he proposed to train me. As the other members of the station staff were all locals, no introductions were necessary.

At that time there were three signalmen, Jim Garland, who lived in one of the station houses with his daughter, Violet, Edgar Smith and Bert Tucker. Jim Garland was a devout Methodist who regularly attended the chapel at Gurney Slade, where his daughter was the organist. He was also a keen amateur astronomer and made use of the night shift to 'star gaze'. Edgar Smith and his wife lived at Binegar arriving at work by bicycle. He was a keen musician and quite a good pianist. Bert Tucker lived at Gurney Slade with his parents, and he too cycled to and from work.

Mrs. Betty Burt was the booking clerk who worked mornings at Binegar and afternoons at Chilcompton, where Stan Ashley was stationmaster. She lived in Gurney Slade and I seem to recall that she was Irish. There were two porters; one of them was Fred Cox, who did alternate early and late turns, and a goods guard Wilf Day, who booked on in time to take the stone train to Evercreech Junction.

A typical day for Norman Down would begin with him arriving in time to see the first 'Down' and the first 'Up' safely on their way, tickets for passengers on these trains having been issued by the early turn porter. Norman would deal with any correspondence that arrived during the day, attend the platform for all passenger trains arriving during his turn of duty, visit the signalbox and inspect for cleanliness, examine the train register and sign it together with the time of his visit.

The locos at that time were the 2P, 3F, 4F, Black Fives, West Country Pacifics, 7F and, of course, the Radstock-based Jintys that banked the freights to Masbury Summit (picking up the tablet and returning 'wrong line'). Any items arriving by passenger or goods train during the hours when there was no clerk on duty would be booked in by Norman, and the necessary postal or telephone advice of their receipt made to the consignee. Likewise, he would deal with items brought to the station for despatch. Heavy items would be weighed by the porter on the platform scales in the goods stores, and light ones on the table top scales in the booking office. At some time during the day he would also check the charges raised by either the porters or the booking clerk for items despatched whilst they were on duty.

Another of Norman's daily duties, carried out in the afternoon, was to enter up all passenger tickets sold, parcels stamps issued, goods invoices raised, and balance the cash taken for these services. A remittance advice would be completed and, together with the appropriate cash, be inserted into a small leather bag and locked in the safe. This bag would be taken out of the safe by him the next day and placed in the travelling safe on either the 6.55am or 8.15am ex-Bath for banking at Dorking. The empty bag, with a receipt, would return at some time the next day.

A further daily chore was to walk round the goods yard, checking that full truck loads received had been booked by the porters, that they were being discharged and, if not, contact the consignee in order to remind them that demurrage charges would be due. Also, in conjunction with the goods yard and Read's

private stone siding, he would compile daily figures of the number and type of wagons received, loaded, unloaded, spare and required. This information would be sent to Bath Control from the signalbox, using the telegraph system, to arrive no later than 10.00am. Later in the day, disposal instructions for spare wagons would be received from control, and these would then be labelled and attached to the appropriate goods train. A daily visit or sometimes a telephone call was also made to Read's private siding to determine the number of wagons required for loading stone, and also the number being despatched later in the day. If my memory serves me correctly, the wagons were weighed in the late morning or early afternoon by being drawn slowly across the weighbridge in a rake. This operation was performed using one of the Radstock 'bankers' crewed by Frank and Jack Kemp, Charlie Rawlings, Wally Moon and Jack Westcombe. Once weighed, the wagons were labelled and shunted into the despatch siding ready for their onward journey later in the day. Read's Quarry had an extension on the eastern side of the A37 road through Gurney Slade. The stone from this was conveyed to the lineside crusher on a tramway with the tubs being clamped to a cableway between the rails. Runaways were an almost daily occurrence!

A typical day's arrivals and despatches through the goods yard could include coal for Bob Steeds of Oakhill, who ran a coal delivery service in the surrounding villages; wheat or barley for the Oakhill Brewery; and cattle feed and feed potatoes (dyed purple to stop them being used for human consumption) for one of the local farmers. The wheat or barley was usually contained in railway sacks, which meant that extra attention had to be paid to them as, when they were eventually returned empty, special rates were used. By this time the wheat and barley for the brewery had to be transported by road as the tramway, which had run from the goods yard to Oakhill, was defunct and had been broken up. My grandfather lost an eye due to a flying steel splinter whilst engaged in dismantling the tramway. The cattle pens were occasionally used but I cannot remember there being much in the way of calf traffic, something that Binegar was once well-known for. Despatches could include lime from Francis Flowers' lime kilns at Gurney Slade, and stone from H. Matthews Quarry, just down the road at Binegar Bottom.

My training as a junior clerk under Norman Down was very thorough. He spent many hours with me, explaining how parcels, small items of goods for the transfer wagons, and full wagon loads were charged. He would appear with a list of various items, their weights and destinations for which I had to work out costs and routes. He would then sit with me afterwards, checking my calculations and, when necessary, explaining where I had gone wrong, and why. The grounding he gave me in the year that I spent at Binegar was to serve me well in the ensuing 17 years that I spent on the railway.

As my service began soon after the war, supplies of stationery were still plentiful. We were issued with pencils which comprised of a piece of tin rolled to take short pencil stubs that would otherwise have been unusable. Our desks had sloping tops and when these pencil holders were allowed to roll down the slope a most satisfactory noise was obtained. Norman Down obviously did not feel the same way about the noise for one morning he came out from his inner office and asked me to bring back a couple of washers after lunch; he intended to silence my noisy pencil.

Whilst he was a kindly man, Norman Down ran the station with a firm hand. On one occasion I went back to the station in the evening to visit the signalbox when Jim Garland was on duty. I was made very welcome, had all the workings of the frame and block instruments explained, and was even allowed to pull a lever or two. However, next morning Norman firmly but politely informed me that the signalbox was 'out of bounds' to unauthorised personnel, and that included me.

In 1947 I was transferred to Evercreech New station to work for stationmaster Bob Hayes. This was due to the sudden increase in traffic generated by Prideaux Milk Foods (Dorsella Milk Powder – Baby Food) and agricultural implements from Jenkins and Gascoigne. There was also a fairly heavy trade in lime from the two lime kilns in the village, Evercreech Lime and Stone Company, and Mead and Sons. At that time the booking clerk was Jim Read; signalmen were Sid Pitt and Frank Trott; porters were Jack Cox and Charlie Hartnell. Jack was an ex-Royal Navy man and was fond of calling out for the benefit of arriving passengers: 'Evercreech New, Evercreech New, over the bridge for Hong Kong, Weihal (or, as he said it, Wee) and Nagasaki!'

Deliveries to the village were by horse and cart 'managed' by George Dyke. Once or twice a week he would be away all day going as far afield as Batcombe and Westcombe.

One lunchtime whilst at the New, I answered a call of nature, when one of the top brass from the Southern

Region, who controlled us at the time, paid a flying visit. Mr. Earle-Edwards was his name. I had locked the office door but had left the key in the lock. By the time I returned the key was in the signalbox and I had to go to Southampton for a reprimand. He was well known for his flying visits and I really should have been more careful.

Full wagons for the goods yard and the private sidings of the two lime companies were collected and delivered by the afternoon 'trip' from Evercreech Junction. Traffic inwards included coal and cattle feed for W. Feaver and Son; culm (small coal) for the two lime companies and raw materials for Jenkins and Gascoigne.

It was whilst I was working at Evercreech that I met the eldest daughter of the joint owner of Mead and Son, who was later to become my wife. After about a year, the trade in milk powder started to drop off and, as a result of this, I became a relief clerk, travelling as far as Shillingstone to the south, Burnham-on-Sea to the west, and Midford to the north.

I recall in those days I smoked a pipe. Whilst on relief at Chilcompton I offered a 'fill' to Stan Ashley, the stationmaster. Imagine my horror as he proceeded to pull out a huge briar four or five times the size of his normal pipe and packed it with the best part of a tin of my 'Bondman'! Not a mistake that I repeated.

Cliff Brown was a clerk at Radstock and was noted for his very untidy desk. When I went there on relief I found the story to be true. However, you could guarantee that he could put his hand on any document asked for without having to search. You tidied his desk at your peril.

In September 1949 I began my two years' National Service in the RAF. Most of my two years was at RAF Watnal, near Nottingham. My journey home on leave was normally from Nottingham LMS to Bristol Temple Meads and thence by Bristol Omnibus to Gurney Slade. My return to camp was by car (a friend) to Bristol to catch the 1.10am Sheffield train from Platform 13. I always travelled in the rear compartment and if awake was very aware of the banker at Bromsgrove (usually Big Bertha) for the ascent of the Lickey Bank. After changing at Derby it was on to Nottingham, usually behind a 2P or a 4F.

It was whilst I was away serving King and country that I found out on my return after being demobbed, there were no positions available to me locally. I was eventually offered a position as a claims and correspondence clerk at Bath Midland Bridge Road, progressing to the accounts section. At that time the goods agent was Fred Marsh, who was well-known on the S&D, followed in turn by A.O. Aburrow, who came from Plymouth. As I lived at Gurney Slade, I was again travelling from Binegar to Bath, using the 7.57am out and the 6.05pm home. It was whilst doing all this travelling that I came to know the Templecombe and Bath guards, Eric Vowles, Dicky Bird and Harold Bromage from Templecombe and Bill (Spitter) Wise, Claude Hickling, Harry Woolley, Roy Woolley, Stan Fishleigh, Jack Simms, Roy Miles, Reg Glass and Archie Cavall, to name just a few; also Walt Adams a travelling ticket collector. I also became quite friendly with one or two loco drivers, Fred Brooks, Stan Bonfield and Frank Hawkins spring to mind. Occasionally, just as the 'right away' was given by the guard when I was travelling home to Binegar on the 6.05pm, I was given the nod to go up and travel on the footplate. Once or twice I was given the shovel and had a go at firing.

Whilst I was at Midland Bridge Road I married and bought a house in Oldfield Park, Bath. I then rented a railway allotment just above Claude Avenue Bridge. My career took me to Bath West goods as a warehouse clerk, then to Bath Spa, first as a booking clerk and later as chief booking clerk. The stationmasters there at that time were Mr. Bray, then Alec Stowe, whilst Paul Pearman had control of Green Park.

In January 1962 I progressed from chief booking clerk to the work study department based in Bristol. After a training period at Paddington, I worked at various locations such as Bristol Temple Meads goods, Avonmouth Docks and Plymouth North Road parcels. I spent 13 months at Plymouth, travelling down on Monday and home on Friday. This period included the very snowy winter of 1963.

In 1964 I left the railway to further my work study 'skills' in private industry but still maintained an interest in railways, particularly steam. During the late 1950s I became a member of Bath Railway Society, later taking over the treasurership from Dick Croft, and, more importantly, met Ivo Peters and Norman Lockett. I had the immense pleasure and privilege of going with Ivo and Norman on many of their photographic expeditions (including some in the Bentley!) at weekends. Other trips to loco sheds with Ivo and Norman were to Nine Elms, Reading South and Gloucester.

On the return journey from a visit to Gloucester we called at the signalbox at Standish Junction. I drew the short straw and was persuaded to see if we could gain access to this 'forbidden territory'. Luckily the signalman was an ex-S&D man that I knew, Walt Woods, so we were in. We also enjoyed a brake van trip from Bath Green Park to Evercreech Junction and visited the Welshpool line when the trains were still running through the streets. A favourite trip was to visit the private railway system at the Bass Brewery in Burton-on-Trent. Here we were conveyed around the extensive system in the Directors' coach behind one of their immaculate engines. The hospitality we received was generous and their excellent product was sampled with relish – Happy Days!

With exhaust drifting away 4F No.44417 coupled to Standard class 4 No.75073 enters Binegar with an express. (*R.E. Toop*)

(*above*) An interlude of time on a cold and snowy scene at Chilcompton station in 1963. It looks like it has been a busy day judging by the number of footprints in the snow on the platform. The signalbox can be seen on the far right. The signalman is probably enjoying a nice hot cup of tea and a warm from the fire. Signalmen who enjoyed their tea at this box include Bill Coombes, Bill Kurton, Norman Rallison, Elijah Oxford and Jack Stacy. (*Keith Barrett collection*)

(*left*) The combination of a class 2P No.40527 and a 4F coasting through Chilcompton on a northbound express. (*SDRT collection*)

(*left*) This summer Saturday formation features 4F No.44422 piloting West Country No.34018 *Axminster* on the down Pines Express consisting of ex-LMS and BR Mark 1 stock, passing Chilcompton in the 1950s. (*SDRT collection*)

(*right*) On the up road, driver Horace (Nobby) Clark is on the ground checking the axle box lubrication, while fireman Wally Moon is on the loco taking on water having banked one train to the top of the Mendips. This was a very exposed location at Chilcompton and even with a frost-fire alongside in the winter it would freeze. The crew always carried cotton waste soaked in paraffin and when needed they set fire to it to free the on-off valve. (*SDRT collection*)

(*left*) Class 4 No.75009 and a 4F No.44417 coming out of Chilcompton Tunnel with the Cleethorpes to Exmouth through train in 1962. (*David Strawbridge collection*)

A gorgeous summer's day at Midsomer Norton in July 1961, as a northbound freight with 2-8-0 7F No.53810 makes its way through the station. (*R.C.Riley*)

(*left*) Porter Les Davies seen here at Midsomer Norton in the 1960s was normally busy around the station. He enjoyed a cigarette whenever the opportunity arose and he was out of sight of the stationmaster. (*Eric Rimmer*)

(*right*) Standard class 4 No. 75071 with a three-coach local train at Midsomer Norton station going towards Bath on 18 May 1963. (*C.L. Caddy*)

(*left*) Blasted trees look on as 8F No.48760 nears Midsomer Norton station on 30 December 1965 with a van for company as it makes its way to Wincanton. (*Authors' collection*)

(*above*) Racing downhill through Midsomer Norton station is Standard 4 No.75071 with a semi-fast Bournemouth to Bristol train in the 1960s. You can now see this signalbox back in all its glory once more thanks to the Somerset & Dorset Railway Heritage Trust. The Trust has done a fantastic job at the station and it is well worth a visit. (*Alan Mitchard*)

(*below*) Cantering into Midsomer Norton station on 16 April 1932 with the Pines Express is class 4F No.4558 heading for Bournemouth. Note the Lux soap powder sign on the right. (*H.C. Casserley*)

(*above*) Working hard up the 1:60 incline through Midsomer Norton station with the southbound LCGB The Wessex Downsman Rail Tour, is class 8F No.48309 on 2 May 1965. (*Alan Mitchard*)

(*below*) Midsomer Norton station on 30 July 1964 shows relief signalman Ivor Patrick in the signalbox with fireman David Humphries returning to Radstock on 0-6-0T 3F No. 47276 for further duties. His regular driver was David Jones who started his railway career in Blackpool and moved home many times due to redundancy. David's son Douglas worked in the loco office in Bath and had been to six different schools before he was eight years old due to his father's movements. (*Keith Barrett collection*)

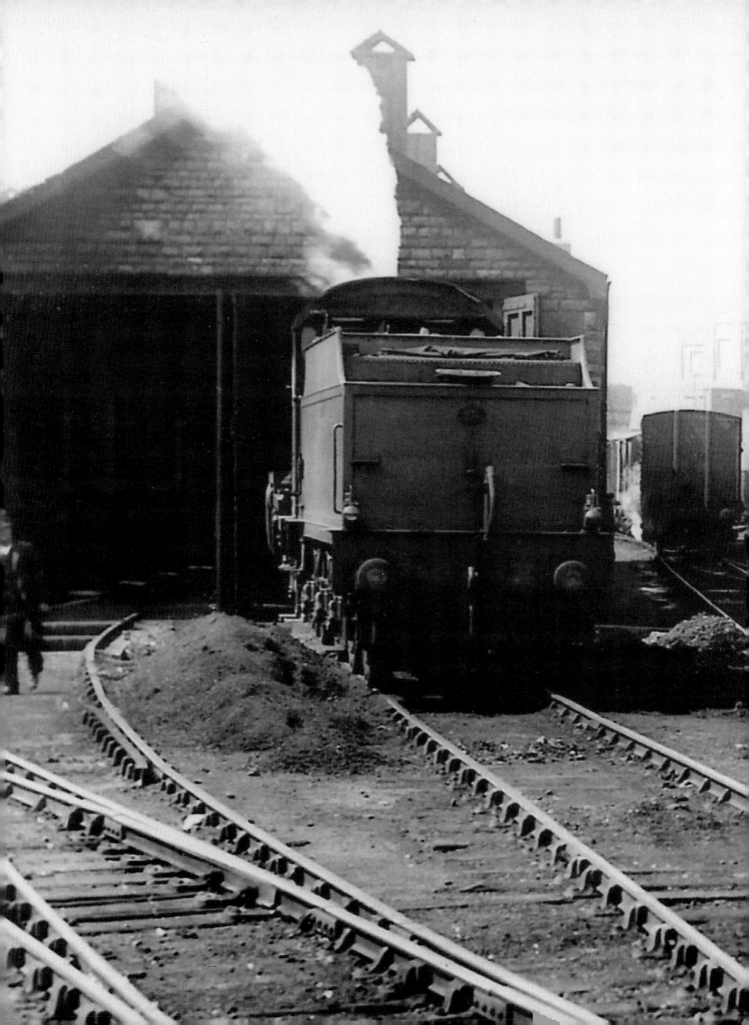

Shunting is in full swing on a bright clear day at Radstock, with 0-6-0 No.59 busy with a string of open and closed wagons, while an unidentified 7F lets off steam on shed, c.1920s. (*R.K. Blencowe collection*)

(*left*) The Kilmersdon Colliery 0-4-0 Saddle Tank shunting engine with driver Herbie Loader in snowy conditions. Radstock railwayman Eric Wilson recalls that the loaded rail coal wagons were coupled to a steel rope and lowered to the GWR (North Somerset line) on a double traverser track; as a loaded wagon travelled down its weight pulled an empty one up with a controlled pulley system. Driver Bert Webster used to have a bit of fun with any new fireman by telling them: 'We have to go up there presently and bring down the coal'. (*SDRT collection*)

(*below*) 7F No.53804 hauling a rake of coal wagons approaching Tyning Bridge from where this photograph was taken in 1956. The resident Jinty Tank engine can just be seen to the left of the signalbox. (*R.K. Blencowe collection*)

(*left*) The railway ambulance teams at each station were highly competitive in tournaments against each other. Here we see the winning Radstock group holding one of the plaques. From left to right are fireman Wally Moon, drivers Aubrey Pearce and Charlie Rawlings with signalman Joe Crouchen. (*Wally Moon collection*)

(*right*) 2P No.632 raises the echoes near Shoscombe with the up Pines Express on 1 April 1935. (*Keith Barrett collection*)

(*left*) Templecombe driver Pat Evans keeps a sharp lookout on Standard class 5 No.73051 on the 9 April 1965, whilst his fireman Maurice Miles is seen having a well earned rest. (*Peter Morton*)

(*left*) Under the watchful eye of the Wellow signalman 4F No.44096 passes the signalbox with a passenger train in 1958. It is photographs like this that make you wish this scene was still with us. (*Norman Simmons/Hugh Davies collection*)

(*below*) On the up Pines are a brace of 2Ps, Nos. 518 and 630, in harness with a passenger train in 1935. The picturesque village of Wellow with the church in the background sets the scene for this lovely photograph. (*Keith Barrett collection*)

(*left*) The pleasant surroundings make this panoramic view even better as 4F No.4271 is on duty with a down slow passenger train near Wellow in August 1934. (*Keith Barrett collection*)

(*right*) Looking very squashed on the footplate of 4-6-0 class 5 No. 73116 are two apprentice fitters, Brian Davis and Eddie Swannack, c.1957. They certainly look too young to be working on the footplate. (*Peter Pike*)

(*left*) What a feast for enthusiasts as LMS 4-4-0s Nos. 699 and 635 with eight coaches on are seen working hard near Wellow on 20 May 1936. (*H.C. Casserley*)

(*right*) Two permanent way staff stand well clear as 9F No.92214 accelerates its three-coach train towards Tucking Mill Viaduct on 22 May 1964. In the background the trackbed of the Camerton Branch can be seen. (*Peter Morton*)

(*left*) On the approach to Midford station in slightly misty conditions is Standard 5 No.73052 with a down local train in the 1960s.
(*Roger Raisey*)

(*right*) Doing the work it was intended to is Standard 4 No.75079 approaching the single-line section at Midford. The absence of the up siding would date this occasion as post-1963. (*Peter Morton*)

(*above*) BR Standard class 4MT No.75073 emerges regally into the sunshine from the south end of Combe Down Tunnel. (*John Yeo collection*)

(*below*) On a damp depressing day 7F No.53807 pilots 4F No.44558 through Lyncombe Vale up towards Combe Down Tunnel. Conditions in the tunnel must have been pretty dire for both crews on that day. (*SDRT collection*)

(*left*) A member of the crew takes a breather as 4F No.4557 is in charge of a three-coach passenger train near Combe Down Tunnel in 1934. (*Keith Barrett collection*)

(*right*) A real close-up of 8F No. 48660 with a down freight, about to pass over Ketley's Bridge (No.11) in Lyncombe Vale in the 1960s. (*Peter Morton*)

(*left*) On 6 January 1964 class 7F No.53806 climbs up through Lyncombe Vale towards Combe Down Tunnel with a goods train and with driver Norman Gibbons at the helm. Note how the spectacle glasses are misted up after going through Devonshire Tunnel. (*Peter Morton*)

(*above*) An afternoon goods train hauled by 7F No.53807 drifts out of Devonshire Tunnel under Maple Grove Bridge and on towards Bath. (*Peter Morton*)

(*right*) On the outskirts of Bath 0-6-0PT class 5700 No.3742 is on banking duties with a heavy freight on 11 August 1964. The photographer is Alan Mitchard. Peter and Alan were schoolboy friends and between them have taken many excellent railway photographs. (*Peter Morton*)

John Tooze

Living in Australia now I often think about my time working at Bath Green Park as a fireman. I recall various stories and characters. One of the senior drivers, Cecil Waldron, was nicknamed 'Smokebox'. When we were on the shed relief turn, it was our duty as firemen to clean the fire. This meant taking up the firebars, around four was the norm. To do this we would take a long-handled shovel which would be about five feet long, which enabled you to reach the front of the firebox. You would then push the fire to the front of the firebox leaving the clinker that would have formed on the firebars. To extract the firebars we used a claw-type firebar tool inserting this between one of the middle bars and levering up four of these bars. We would then bring them onto the footplate, and break up any clinker from the back of the firebox with a clinker bar. This would then be shovelled down through the gap where the firebars had been removed, through to the ashpan where the driver would be standing in the ashpit raking out the clinker. If the engine was due to go out again later, the fireman would shovel back the best of the fire from the front to the back of the firebox and also clean the front of the firebox of clinker. The fireman would then shovel coal on to the fire, keeping the engine in steam, although by now steam pressure would have dropped. But there would still be enough steam to move the engine back into the shed. One of the other duties was to clear the smokebox of fire ash which could build up as high as the blast pipe. This is where the driver, Cecil Waldron, would always say to the fireman: 'Don't forget the smokebox'; hence his nickname. He was also a pipe smoker and he was forever tapping out his pipe. Those of us senior firemen who were brazen enough would say when knocking off duty: 'Don't forget to clean out the ash from your pipe, Cecil'. It was all taken in good fun.

Charlie Morrish, nicknamed 'Waterbaby', was a senior driver in what we called The Tankie Link. This was where a 2P Tank loco was used on passenger work, such as trips to Bristol Temple Meads. We would come on duty at 5.10am and prepare the engine, the driver would oil all the necessary oil points and check around the loco to see that everything was in order for the trip, while the fireman would be making up his fire. Usually these locos were already coaled up and always standing on the top pit which was next

to the turntable. Other duties for the fireman were to check there was a full tin of detonators, two red flags and five spanners of various sizes, fill the sand boxes and ensure the smokebox door was shut tight. Then we would wait for the signalman to give us the signal to pull away from the shed over on to the back road, where we would fill up the water tank. From memory this would be something like 2,500 gallons, which was more than enough for the trip to Bristol Temple Meads, where we always topped up again for the return trip to Bath Green Park. When the water tank had been filled, the fireman would go down to the messroom to make a brew of tea to take with him. During this time the loco would have been blowing off steam, and the water level gauge would have dropped very slightly. This was no real problem as it was always enough for the trip to Bristol T.M. But driver Charlie Morrish always insisted we topped up the water again before going off shed and down to Bath Green Park station to pick up our train. So he was given the nickname 'Waterbaby'.

We used to shunt and pick up at Moorewood Sidings stone quarry. The mother of Bill Rawles, one of our drivers, lived alongside the railway line where we would do the shunting. It was the practice of most S&D men that when you were shunting there, you would roll off lumps of coal for her in the winter months. On one occasion a crew did just that. But the embankment from the railway track to her back garden was very steep and a rather large boulder of coal was pushed off the footplate gathering speed as it rolled down the bank. Unfortunately on this occasion it went crashing through the garden fence and demolished her shed completely. Poor old Bill had the job of building his mother a new garden shed with help from some of the S&D lads. The new shed was built further down the garden this time. This I found to be true because a few days later, we were shunting at that same siding and saw the carnage. It was all taken with good humour and Bill came in for a bit of ribbing by all, as you can imagine.

Driver Reg Beasley was very much the devilment type, he was always up for funny tricks. He and his fireman were on a return goods trip one day from Evercreech Junction to Bath. After shunting at Shepton Mallet it was the usual thing to top up the water tank. The engine they were using was a class 2-8-0 7F. His fireman had put the water bag in the tender and when it was full, Reg said to his fireman:

'Don't bother getting back up on the tender to take the bag out'. Reg's idea was to draw the train away at a slow pace, thinking that the bag would slide out as he drew the train away. Unfortunately, instead, he pulled the water column down; consequently water went sky high everywhere. What had happened was that the water column bags were made of leather and were in two or three sections and secured around with metal studs. This one was made in three sections and the third section join got caught up on the inside rim of the tender water tank, pulling the thing over. Reg was naturally on the carpet on the Monday morning. He never attempted this sort of prank again.

steam pressure as we needed a full head of steam from the bottom of Bitton Bank to Oldland Common, as it was a steady incline. We had between 35 and 40 wagons on. Running in on the up loop the engine would be detached and we would cross over the main line to the down goods, where we would have around a 30-minute break whilst our train was being made up for our return journey to Bath. This turn of duty was worked in two parts, leaving Bath at 11.29pm on the first journey and again at 2.30am from Bath to Westerleigh, then back to Bath and into the shed. It was a daunting experience that I will never forget, to have been in a responsible position, especially being

It is 1962 and type 4 Peak class No.D106 is the first diesel-hauled Pines Express from Manchester seen here at Bath Green Park. In the cab are driver Dick Evry, on the left, with John Tooze. Do any of the young railway enthusiasts recognise themselves? (*John Tooze collection*)

My first driving turn came three weeks after passing out for driving duties. I had just come on duty for the 10.30pm spare. What had happened was that the night shift foreman called in sick, so the booked driver for the 11.29pm goods to Westerleigh took over the foreman's duties; therefore the driving position became my first driving turn. This was normal practice of seniority. The foreman came down to the messroom and said I was to drive the goods to Westerleigh which was over the Midland line. Starting from Bath up goods yard through Weston, Bitton, Oldland Common, Warmley, Mangotsfield North, on to Westerleigh Sidings which was rather a big shunting yard. On entering this yard my experience as a fireman stood me in good stead; also as a fireman I had good experience of firing this type of engine which was a 7F. I was able to maintain

on a night shift as things look different then, as we all know. Returning from Westerleigh we would be running tender first. This could be a miserable trip in cold wet weather, as all we had protecting us from the elements was a storm sheet fitted over the cab and on to the tender, tied down with ropes to keep it secure. But all went well, and the experience of my fireman was appreciated in him maintaining steam pressure.

My memories of drivers I fired to along the way are mainly of good blokes such as George Tucker with whom I am still in contact, Ern Hemmings, Bill Rawles, Len West, Harold Burford, Dennis Latham, Fred Shipp, Vic Hunt, Dick Evry, Charlie Hamilton, Harold Barber, Edgar Gray, Ron Gray, Vic Ball, Harry Waldron, Harry Starkey, Fred Love and many, many more.

Making their way across the girder bridge at Bath Green Park are pilot engine 2P No.40563 with driver Charlie Gould and LMS class 4 2-6-0 No.43036 (nicknamed Doodlebug) with a southbound express in August 1950. (*H.F.Wheeller/ R.S. Carpenter collection*)

A double-headed northbound express running into Bath Green Park behind an unidentified 4-4-0 2P and Standard 5 with an eleven-coach train of Mk1 stock. (*SDRT collection*)

Gordon King

I come from a long line of railwaymen. My great-grandfather was an engine driver at Cardiff, my grandfather was head fitter at Highbridge Locomotive Works and my father was Arthur James King, an engine driver. His brother Charlie was a driver at Highbridge and another brother Harold worked at the carriage works at Swindon. My eldest brother, Arthur William King, was also an S&D driver. I worked at Bath Green Park as a fireman for some time before joining British Transport Police in 1951 and my daughter Josephine Victoria King worked as a secretary in the engineering department at Temple Meads station, Bristol.

I was born at Edithmead, just north of Highbridge, where my father was working as a passed fireman. We moved to Bath in June 1939 when my father was promoted to a driver. We lived in a house a stone's throw from the S&D loco shed. In September 1939, my brother Arthur and I were called up with our Territorial Unit when war was declared but after a while Arthur was transferred to the Royal Engineers and spent the rest of the war driving MoD engines in Britain, North Africa and Italy.

When I was discharged from the army I went to work on the railway. I worked in the office of the running shed with foreman Arthur Polden. One day he asked me to pass him a drawing pin which he then proceeded to push into his leg. I did not know at this time that Arthur had an artificial leg; he lost his leg in an accident on his first day as a fireman. Apparently this was a favourite trick of his. I then worked as a cleaner and later as a fireman.

I remember one day working with driver Fred Epps on a goods train to Evercreech Junction. When we went over the top of the Mendips at Masbury I applied the engine handbrake as usual, but after a while we seemed to be going too fast and no matter what Fred did it was apparent that the train was out of control. I must point out at this stage that the engine on a 7F class freight was fitted with the experimental Ferodo brake blocks. Engine brake blocks were made of cast iron and very soon were worn out through excessive use on the 1 in 50 gradients over the Mendips. The Ferodo Company was trying to make the brake blocks out of a composite material which would last longer than the one or two days it was then. Fred opened the whistle and kept it open to warn the signalman what was happening. When we got to Evercreech New it was obvious that

we were not going to stop at Evercreech Junction and we did in fact think about jumping off the engine, but both of us decided to stay. When we got within sight of the Junction, we saw a goods train backing up from the station on to the Highbridge branch line. Luckily for us the train was clear when we arrived at Evercreech but unfortunately the line gates were closed at the station. The signalman saw that we were not going to stop and opened them up in time for us to pass through safely. We managed to stop some miles down the line where we found that most of the brake blocks had disintegrated. The Ferodo Company did later manage to perfect the blocks, saving a lot of time and money.

Another incident I remember was when we were taking a train load of RAF bombs which were going to be dumped at sea after the war. As we approached Chilcompton I looked back and saw flames coming from one of the trucks. I told my driver and he stopped at Chilcompton station and I went back to see what was wrong. I found that an axle box on the wagon was on fire and the wooden side was also alight. I saw that the wagon had grease axle boxes; loads of this type should have been loaded in trucks with oil-filled axle boxes. The guard joined me and I signalled to the driver to draw ahead and we placed the truck under the water column, which is used to fill engine tenders with water, and extinguished the fire. When we got to Evercreech Junction this truck was removed from the train. On our return to Bath we were told that Mr. A. Whitaker, the shed superintendent, wanted us. We went to his office and he thanked us for what we had done and said we had probably saved the village of Chilcompton and the surrounding district from being obliterated.

Another incident I well remember was when I was firing to a driver, whom I shall call F, on a goods train to Birmingham. It was a very foggy night and the engine was not steaming well as the coal in the bunker was just a load of dust. We were stopped at a signal the other side of Cheltenham and driver F got off the engine and said to me: 'When you do manage to get any steam you can catch me up'. I worked on the fire and managed to get a full head of steam just as the signal came off for us to go. At the time I was not very experienced but I was determined not to show this and I drove the train very slowly, looking out for the driver. After about 10 minutes I saw him still walking and slowed down for him to join the train. He got on the engine and in fact I don't think he said another word for the rest of the journey or on the return journey. I did however get some satisfaction some years later when as a Police Officer I was asked by the running shed foreman Tommy Rudd to remove a driver from the shed as he was drunk. It was then that I saw it was driver F on an engine and he was refusing to get off. I got onto the footplate and told him in no uncertain manner that either he left the premises and went home or I would lock him up. I reminded him that being in charge of an engine while drunk was a very serious offence which carried a prison sentence and dismissal. Tommy Rudd said he did not want me to arrest him, just remove him. This I did, feeling a little satisfaction for the way he had treated me before.

I was lucky to be stationed at Bath when I joined the Transport Police. Part of our beat was the S&D line down to Templecombe and Highbridge. We also policed the GWR line from Swindon to Keynsham and to Westbury. I remember receiving a call one day that a person had been knocked down at Keynsham. After a thorough search I found a handbag and part of a jawbone. This I took to the local dentists. One of them remembered filling a tooth and he told me who this had belonged to. The name matched details found in the handbag so we were able to positively identify the victim. I dealt with numerous other cases of accidents and suicides; these were often not very nice to handle as an engine can make an awful mess of a human body.

There were also funny cases as well as tragic ones. I can recall once having to break down the door of a toilet of the Pines Express which arrived at Bath Green Park with a lady locked in it.

At one time we received numerous reports of theft from the goods depot at Bath Green Park and although we kept watch we never caught the person. I studied the rosters of railwaymen who had been on duty when things were stolen and concluded that it was an old engine driver who worked on the local shunter. I had a quiet word in his ear and told him in no uncertain manner that if anything went missing again I knew where to come. Nothing else went missing from the shed but we could never prove anything against him.

One of our biggest troubles was with the Teddy Boys during the 1950s. At this time I had a police dog called Tina (*pictured right, with Gordon King*) and when we had some trouble one Friday evening I rounded up about 20 of them with Tina and locked them up. The next morning the lady magistrate said that the police should have more dogs as they appeared to be very effective.

I can remember being at Stapleton Road station when we had trouble with football hooligans. As we were running to catch them, one of the police dogs took a bite out of my leg. I think this was because I was in plain clothes and not in uniform.

I worked on the Royal Train and on one occasion when the Duke of Edinburgh arrived he was met by the Lord Lieutenant of Avon, Sir John Wills. As they came towards me Sir John said to the Duke: 'Mr. King used to be my Sergeant Major'. The Duke looked at the three stripes on my arm and said: 'I see you have been demoted then'. I must add that when I was in the Territorial Army Sir John was my Colonel.

On another occasion when the Duke was visiting the School of Infantry at Warminster I was waiting with some of my men for his return on Warminster station. It had been raining very hard for some time and we were all very wet indeed. The Duke looked at us and said: 'You lads look as if you could do with a stiff drink'. A minute or two later the Duke's steward came from the train with a drink of whisky for all of us. Of course we had to refuse as we were not allowed to drink on duty but who could refuse a Royal Command? I always enjoyed working on the S&D and was glad to still work there as a police officer.

103

8F No.48309 toiling up the bank towards Devonshire Tunnel with a LCGB special, the Wessex Downsman Rail Tour in the 1960s. (*Peter Morton*)

(*above*) Fred Holmes who originally came from the Midlands was a driver and running foreman at Bath Green Park. His daughter recalls that 7F No.53809 always seemed to develop faults; his favourite 7F was No.53806. (*Nancy Holmes*)

(*left*) Fireman Ronald Bath seen here on 9 December 1947, aged 22. He started his career at Bath Green Park in 1943. He then went to Birmingham and returned to Bath in 1956. (*Brenda Griffin collection*)

(*right*) On the last day of service on 5 March 1966, the crew for the 16.37 down train have their farewell photograph taken at Bath. In the cab, from left to right, are driver George Welch, fireman Bruce Briant and on the platform is guard Reg Brewer next to a young lad, who wants to be part of this historic photograph. (*John Stamp*)

(*below*) Passenger guard Roy Miles, who was a smashing fellow, surveys the gardens at Bath Green Park station. We wonder if Roy did any weeding before taking out his next train to Bournemouth West? (*Lesley Miles collection*)

(*above*) Two old friends are enjoying a chat in the sunshine at Bath Green Park station. Porter Bert Ilott is on the left with guard Charlie Davies, who is about to take out a Bournemouth train. (*Vince Henderson collection*)

(*below*) Looking work-stained and in need of a clean is 2-8-0 7F No.53806 at Bath Green Park in the 1960s. In the cab are footplate crew Fred Love (left) and Jim Machin. (*Peter Morton*)

(*left*) On 11 August 1964 BR Standard 5 No.73051 on the 09.55 Bath to Bournemouth with a train of three LMS coaches and a GUV, skirts Bellotts Road before crossing the Western Region by means of Bridge No.3. (*Peter Morton*)

(*right*) Stanier 8F No.48309 stands in Bath Green Park station at the head of the Wessex Downsman Rail Tour in May 1965. Everybody is taking their last photographs before boarding the train to Bournemouth. (*David Walden*)

(*left*) Class 4F No.44264 heads a special train into Bath Green Park, while an 8F No.48309 is waiting to take the train over the Somerset and Dorset to Bournemouth in the 1960s. (*Alan Mitchard*)

A Railway Family

Richard Gunning

Railways, and the Somerset and Dorset in particular, have always been part of my life. My father's family were woven into the S&D through their employment. Also my parent's friends were mostly railway families, so my childhood was dominated by railway life, not to mention living by the line in Bath. Even my secondary school in Brougham Hayes was within sight of Green Park Loco and next to the Western main line. In my later years my interest in all things railway has remained.

My Dad, Archie, and his two older brothers, Bill and Tom, were all drivers at Green Park, while my grandfather Emmanuel was a ganger in the Bath permanent way gang. Bill's son Reg also began his railway career on the footplate on the S&D during the war. Even some of my friends were employed there for a short time in the 60s.

As a boy, I remember life with the S&D. At home, I had to live with Dad leaving for work at all hours, and being in bed at all times of the day. Mum would say: 'Sshh, your Dad's asleep, don't wake him', and I learnt to be quiet. We even wrapped an old sock around the front door knocker – lest someone, not in the know, would call and disturb his sleep by rattling the knocker. We lived in Oldfield Park, near the S&D's climb to Devonshire Tunnel and the passing of the trains became almost unnoticeable, but you could set your watch by them, well at least the passenger trains. Incredibly we knew a train was imminent as the door in the kitchen always rattled when a train was climbing up the bank. In later years, I never understood this, as we lived some distance from the bank. Mum and Dad would socialise with long-term railway friends, and I was always fascinated by the talk and anecdotes of various people whom we would meet.

Dad began his career at Bath Green Park Loco in 1929, and remained there during World War II as he was employed in a reserved occupation, and footplate staff were chosen for service on a random basis. This meant he was passed for driving at an early age. His LMS record sheet shows this was on 10 February 1941, when he was 28 years old. He was only promoted to driver after the war, and also by completing the magical '626 driving turns'. He always formed great friendships with his mates, both when firing and driving. Some

of those firemen I remember were Ron Bean, Ken Coffin, John Tooze, Jim (Digger) Hillier, Brian Smith, and Dave Massey. He progressed through the links, and finally made it to the top link in 1964, as his ex-driver and long-term mate Dick Evry retired, and he took his place. In 1966 he was offered the chance to transfer to Bristol Bath Road Diesel Depot, when the S&D closed. His seniority would have placed him in number 2 link, which I think was the 'Derby Link', but he chose to leave the railway. However, once a long-term railway-man always a railwayman and he eventually saw out the final years before retirement in the permanent way gang on the WR mainline. He enjoyed his life on the S&D, and had some great fun, despite the dirt, dust, cold, rain, unsociable hours and all the other less glamorous aspects of footplate life. I remember his regular visits to Bath Eye Infirmary, as it was then, to extract foreign bodies from his eyes, mainly coal dust.

Nearly everyone at the Loco, and beyond, had nicknames and Dad was usually one of the ones who thought them up. There were many characters at Green Park and usually their nicknames reflected this.

During the war a Home Guard establishment was formed from those operating the S&D. Dad always used to liken it to the TV programme *Dad's Army*, and could see the funny side of organising the home defence. Tales of one rifle between 20 men on marches to Hinton Charterhouse, a village near Wellow, for practice with firearms that usually ended in disaster and a retreat to the local pub was necessary. A large number of Admiralty staff moved to Bath to escape the London bombing, and they too had a Home Guard unit. An exercise was held once in which the Admiralty unit was to act as the enemy, whilst the S&D contingent was to defend Green Park depot. Needless to say the more professional attitude of the Admiralty won the day. A chalk mark on each locomotive door signified they had been 'captured' by the enemy. Every engine was captured and Dad, on sentry duty on Victoria Bridge Road, was 'overrun' by the enemy, by not taking things too seriously.

Dad's LMS record sheet shows a few misdemeanours during the war. Late on duty, on early mornings, and failing to keep a look out on other

Archie Gunning in the cab of class 3 Tank No.82004 on the 8.15am Bath to Templecombe train in the summer of 1965. (*Richard Gunning collection*)

occasions, which required a trip to Derby to see the feared Colonel Rudguard for a disciplinary hearing.

He told me a long tale about taking a class 5XP Jubilee up to Combe Down Tunnel in the wartime, when he was a passed fireman to Dick Evry. The pair were in the S&D goods link and on this occasion were returning from Evercreech Junction. They were about to rush off early after disposing of their engine, in order to get in a quick pint at the *Newbridge Inn* before it closed. They were stopped doing so by the shedmaster and told to relieve a crew on an incoming train from the north at the station. When they reached the loco which had come in from the north, they were told that the train was overloaded for two engines for the journey south over the S&D. I seemed to remember that Dad spoke of 14 vehicles, which was I suppose not uncommon during the war. As the regular banker was having its fire cleaned, and not available, they were asked to bank the train to the Combe Down Tunnel with an engine that had brought the train in. Having been thwarted in their efforts to have a quick pint, they didn't give the request too much thought, and accepted that their efforts to finish early were gone and just got on the loco without even looking at it. Halfway up the bank Dad was on his seat in the cab and looked behind. Normally looking back he would see the boiler, as they were tender first. He was astounded to see a nameplate and asked Dick what engine they had; they both realised it was a 5XP, which was banned on the line (I think because of axle weight). Dick in typical fashion decided to carry on and hoped to get

away with it. Needless to say they didn't and both he and Dad were fined three days' loss of pay for using a loco which was banned over the line.

After promotion to driver after the war, things settled down and he worked his way through the various links and generally that's how I remember him, as a goods link driver.

In May 1960 the BBC *Railway Roundabout* programme decided to produce a film of an S&D goods train for a feature. They selected the 11.00 am goods train from Bath to Evercreech Junction. By luck Dad and his mate Brian Smith were working that turn on the week of the filming. Both were given new overalls to wear for the occasion and given special instructions on how to behave! He played it down, but was secretly looking forward to the big day. 7F No. 53807, then I think the best of its class, was 'spruced up', even with a brand new fire bucket, new tools and given the once over by the fitters. Inspector Dowell from Gloucester rode on the train, which was especially made up for the day. The filmmakers also requested that a class 7 was to be provided for banking the train up to Combe Down Tunnel. One was prepared by the relief crew, and an argument developed between them and the rostered banking crew from the junction sidings over who was to man this engine. Both hoped for stardom as the cameras rolled and it was only the intervention of Mr. Harold Morris, the shedmaster, who was able to resolve the dispute! After the eager anticipation of the screening, my Mum thought Dad had been trying to get himself on screen as much as possible

S&D railwaymen going out for a Christmas drink in 1965. From left to right are Ron Bryant, George Trevor, Ray Russell, Harry Shearn, Richard and Archie Gunning. (*Richard Gunning collection*)

and played to the cameras. Of course, the resulting *Railway Roundabout* video has been available for some years.

Dad also drove the last up Pines Express from Bath northwards to Gloucester. The 12 coaches brought into Bath by 9F No.92220 *Evening Star*, had to be taken singlehandedly, with nothing more than a Black Five, as in 1962 the diagrams were altered and the usual Peak Diesel took the following relief. A regular passenger in the train gave Dad a *Thomas the Tank Engine* postcard with a thank-you message (which I still have) and ten shillings (50p) to share with his mate.

Talking of diesels, I remember that when he was promoted to the top link he had to be trained on the Peak Class and also had to learn the road to Birmingham New Street Station. This was for the 10.15pm parcels and the return from Landore Street Junction with the 12.17am Leicester to Bath parcels. He borrowed my Uncle Bill's handbook with all the signals laid out in sequence over this route, and I remember painstakingly making a copy for him, whilst revising for my 'O' level exams. The parcels was a good turn for Dad, usually with overtime or mileage payments and it was looked forward to, even though it was nights. He soon learnt to appreciate the diesels, and enjoyed a new way of working, although he was caught out by the new power that he had available. I remember him telling me that uncontrolled acceleration had brought the speed up to 60mph by the time he reached Weston station once or twice, when his train was limited to 45mph!

Dave Massey was his very last fireman in this link, and he would let Dave have a go at driving this new traction. Diesel reliability even at this time was not good and you could always tell if he had a 'steamer' substitute when he returned home in the morning – he was not in a good mood. He enjoyed the diesels with their warm and comfortable cabs. It was so good one night, that while waiting in the loop at Abbotswood, both he and Dave fell asleep and had to be woken up by the signalman.

So to the end of his footplate career in 1966 and the closure of the S&D. In the final week he worked the 8.15am passenger to Templecombe and the 2.00pm back to Bath. On the final Sunday he and his brother Bill were rostered for the SLS special to Bournemouth Central and back. He told me once, he hadn't signed for the road from Branksome to Central Station, but his brother on the train engine knew the road and he, in effect, shepherded the train in this section (totally illegally).

* * *

Tom Gunning joined the railway as a callboy and messenger in the mid 1920s. On nights he walked to the railwaymen's houses to wake them up for their early morning turns, and in the daytime he would run messages. After a period of time he was transferred to Highbridge where he lodged with a widow who kept pigs. Later on he did a spell at Walsall with his two pals Vic Towers and Norman Gibbons.

Tom met his wife Joyce in the buffet at Bath Green Park station where she worked. He became a fireman

A very dapper guard, who could be Bill Wise, with Joyce Russell, who worked in the buffet at Bath Green Park station. Joyce later married driver Tom Gunning. (*Pauline Keen collection*)

Photographed in the 1930s at Bath Green Park station are, from left to right, driver Ralph Holden (senior), fireman Harold Barber and Joyce Russell. (*Pauline Keen collection*)

in the mid 1930s and was passed for driving during the war. During this period he told the story of ammunition trains in the sidings during the blitz on Bath in 1942. While the bombs were dropping, Tom and his mate would shelter under the train, completely forgetting about their dangerous load.

During the war beer was in short supply. Trains containing beer from the Midlands still ran. One bright spark devised a way to relieve a part of this precious cargo through a tube connected to the barrels in the wagons; this soon spread around the S&D.

Tom was a few years older than Dad and stood about ten places in seniority over him. Although a conscientious railwayman he was different to both Dad and Bill as he always had a carefree attitude to life, nothing seemed to faze him. I always got on well with him, from the time he gave me footplate rides as a ten-year-old. Unfortunately his eyesight deteriorated and he was pronounced unfit for mainline

duties. He became a 'green carder', and took up a position in the shed and shunting link. When closure was announced, he opted to transfer to Bristol Bath Road Depot where, lo and behold, this all-diesel depot allowed him to return to the main line where driving with glasses was allowed. So in one short step he moved from the mundane shunting and loco preparation to going straight to the top link at Bath Road to drive prestigious trains such as the Blue Pullman. Talk about chalk and cheese!

Tom was not a young man when he transferred and had an enormous task in learning all the various routes associated with his new depot, not to mention the variety of diesel traction types he would have to drive. This mission did not outwardly trouble him and it is to his credit that he stuck to the task. He retired in the mid 80s and enjoyed the pleasures of his retirement – a few pints and, of course, the odd flutter on the gee-gees!

* * *

It is 1953 and it is the Railway Children's Christmas party at the Railway Club, Lower Bristol Road, Bath. Some who attended the party are family members, Barbara, Pauline, John and Richard Gunning. How many others recognise themselves? (*Pauline Keen collection*)

Bill Gunning was the eldest of the three brothers on the footplate at Green Park Loco and was in a firing job when he used to give Dad rides as a young boy. He was very influential on Dad and perhaps this was the reason Dad followed him into a railway career. Bill's son Reg was also part of the railway family, but left Bath for promotion to one of the Bristol Sheds. Towards the end of Bill's career he became senior driver at Green Park and retired on the closure of the shed in April 1966.

* * *

My memory of my own first interest in railways was asking Dad to write down all the numbers of the locomotives at Green Park Depot. I suppose I was about six or seven years old. From there I graduated to collecting numbers and after a while had seen all the locomotives of the S&D, so I started trainspotting on the Western mainline. As I got older my friends and I (we all had railway privilege tickets, as our fathers were railwaymen) ventured further afield to Bristol, Birmingham, Salisbury, Southampton, Cardiff and the

famed trainspotting site at Tamworth. London was an occasional visit usually accompanied by an adult.

My favourite place however was Templecombe to see the Southern mainline locomotives, but the fascination of the S&D workings always held our interest. We caught the 8.15am local from Bath and usually being the only passengers, at least in our coach, we would open all the windows as we approached Devonshire Tunnel. The effect of the loco's exhaust in that confined space, I am sure can be imagined. Needless to say, the guard of the train was not very happy with us, but then again, we probably knew him as a friend of my father and got away with a mild rebuke.

Summer Saturdays in the late 1950s and early 1960s brought a wide variety of through traffic to Green Park, and attracted hordes of local spotters to Victoria Bridge Road to trespass by the side of the Midland Yard Shunter's Cabin, in order to catch the 'cops' of the locos from sheds far away up north. Invariably we were thrown out and had to watch from the road below.

Richard Gunning's favourite footplate ride on a Saturday morning at the Junction sidings in the winter of 1961. On this day they didn't have the usual 4F No.44146. Instead it was a Jinty (known by Richard and his friends as a Bagnall) which was unusual on this roster. The fireman in the cab is Jim (Digger) Hillier. (*Richard Gunning collection*)

With Dad as a driver though, I was able to extend my interest through various footplate rides he was able to give me. On bank holidays and occasional Sundays we moved the locos around the shed. As a young lad Dad would take me to the shed to collect his pay if he was working nights. After which he would take me over to the signalbox where Bill Wilds the signalman would allow me to pull some levers. A regular footplate ride was on the returning 2.10pm 'engine and van' trip to Westerleigh Sidings. This train would arrive back at the junction sidings just after 7.00pm. So after tea, I would walk to Victoria Bridge Road, up to the track, walk across the running lines, and jump up on the footplate. Usually it was an S&D class 7F but latterly in 1962/63 a Stanier class 8F. Thereafter a good hour's shunting was had, mostly with me driving. We then returned to the shed to dispose of the engine and as these rides usually took place in the summer, Dad would push his bike along to the *Royal Oak* pub, which was situated by the S&D, where I would have lemonade and a packet of crisps and he would have a pint. Off we would go home to bed, ready for me to face school next day.

Green Park Loco was a great place on Sundays. There was no one in authority to be seen and it was open house to us spotters. There were very few 'cops' but we had a wonderful time climbing over the engines, pretending we were driving the Pines Express.

Undoubtedly my favourite excursion on the footplate was the junction sidings banker. Dad was on this turn on Saturday mornings about every eight weeks during the winter service from about 1958 to 1963. Oh, how I would look forward to this event. We shunted the yard, transferred wagons to Midland Bridge Road Depot, and went to the Stothert and Pitt private sidings and the Bath Gas Works sidings. Banking became less and less as the years went by and loads decreased, but there was still enough activity. Dad's fireman would usually retire to the shunter's cabin for a game of 'Benny' (a bizarre card game, allegedly invented in Green Park Loco man's cabin!), and it was me doing the driving and occasionally the firing, watched over by Dad. I soon learnt not to snatch the couplings of the wagons as we pulled rakes of wagons in and out of different sidings. The shunters' hand signals were difficult to follow at first, but they all knew I was driving and made allowances for my mistakes. Gus Beeho was the leading shunter, and he understood my youthful exuberance. Sometimes Dad would pop over to Frank Bealing's on the Lower Bristol Road to have his hair cut, which would leave his fireman and me on the footplate. The shunters were always quite happy to let me get on with it. I remember Armstrong 4F No.44146 as being my favourite engine. Later on, however, it went to Derby for an overhaul and thereafter was used on the main line. When the Western Panniers were transferred to Green Park, I always hoped we would have one on this turn, but it was never to be.

With the loss of the through express over the S&D in 1962 and the onset of other interests that go with a teenage boy growing up, my day-to-day trainspotting and visits to the S&D slowly drifted away. The line was running down and I began work, and although the railway still dominated family life, I paid little interest and did other things with my life.

As the end of the S&D approached our family's mood became very sombre. It was the end of life as we had known it for so many years and it was going to be a big upheaval. This must have affected many railwaymen who were in these circumstances. Although I had lost interest Dad tried to persuade me to take one last trip with him over the S&D during the line's last week of existence. I remember I had a few days' holiday, which I could have taken, but decided that I was too busy doing other things. Mum told me I would regret it one day – how right she was. I ignored most of what was going on, preoccupied with other things.

On the final Sunday, 6 March 1966, Dad and his brother worked the last return train over the S&D, but again I declined his offer to take a trip. They arrived back in Bath about 6.30pm in the evening. A neighbour realised the significance to Dad and told me he was going to Green Park station to see the final scenes, and suddenly the penny dropped for me and I realised what was about to happen. I went with him to the station where Dad's train had already arrived, amid the huge crowds of enthusiasts and locals who had come to witness the end of an era. There were a

great many photographs being taken, and Dad and my uncle and their mates were asked to sign autographs. Soon it was all over and the locomotives had to be returned to the shed and as many of us as possible climbed on to the footplates of both engines. Dad said to me: 'You can drive', and at that moment all my boyhood memories of riding on footplates with Dad came flooding back. I jumped into the driver's seat of class 8F No.48706 and spun the reverser into backward gear and yanked open the regulator. It was all over in a flash, back to the depot, where Dad's regular fireman, Dave Massey, was acting as the final day Running Foreman. We turned the loco on the turntable and dropped down over the pit, but there was no need to put the loco under the coal chute this time – she wouldn't be moving again.

That is where the railway family ended in effect and I have been looking back to those days of my youth ever since, especially every time my wife and I visit Sainsbury's in Bath. I do like to tell her the story of how I was the very last person to drive a locomotive in Green Park station! After all this time she still believes I am making it up.

BR Standard class 4MT No.76057 waits for departure from Bath Green Park. The fireman seems to have a problem with the locomotive lamps and the engine could do with a clean. (*Keith Barrett collection*)

Bath Green Park shed with Standard 4-6-0 No.73049 blowing off steam. Shed labourer George Williams looks like he has been hard at work with the very large shovel that he is holding. *(R.K. Blencowe collection)*

A nostalgic photograph of S&DJR office staff taken in the 1920s at No.14 Green Park Buildings, Bath. This photograph has been seen before but thanks to Keith Baker and Tim Deacon we have now found most of the names. We feel this is such an important part of S&D history and well worth all the extra effort in finding the staff names. From left to right, the back row includes Arthur Townsend, Charlie Spencer, Len Hazzard and George Quinn. The second row down includes Stan Ashford, Bob Perkins, Ted Ashford, Harold Barry and Fred Frankling. The third row down includes Bert Hazzard, Jack Loader, Bill Durston, Arthur Sharman, Fred Marsh, Reg Pow, Jack Thomas, Ern Keyes, Chas Hunt, Tom Chamberlain, Ivor Durston, Sid Sealey, Gerald Osbourne, Percy Ingram, Reg Ashford, Vic Pitman, Fred Marsh, George Trowbridge and Chris Edwards. The fourth down includes Ned Marsh, Bill Hackwood, Ted Haskins, Mr. Jackson, Harry Hackwood, Albert Chamberlain, Frank Maggs, A.R. Collier (chief accountant), G.H. Wheeler (superintendent of the line), T. Draper, G.H. Eyre (ex-superintendent of the line), Jack Thomas, Eric Steger, Bob Hackwood and John Barry. The front row includes Frank Kelvill, Bill Price, Bill Comley, Stan Newman, Diana Maginn, Gwen Gillingham, Mr. Coombes, Fred Cross, Joe Chamberlain, Frank Cross and Edgar Pothecary. (*Keith Baker collection*)

(*above*) 3F 0-6-0 No.3260 stands next to the engine shed at Bath on 17 May 1936. This is the engine that collided with a peat train down on the branch near Ashcott. It was derailed and plunged into the south drain. It was not considered to be recoverable and was scrapped where it lay. (*H.C. Casserley*)

(*below*) The magnificent frontage of Bath LMS and S&D station, so in keeping with the local architecture, and what a wonderful display of travel posters on the boards outside. Also look at the vehicles of the day, they set the date for this 1930s photograph. (*Richard Dagger collection*)

(*above*) With plenty of steam on show is 2-6-2T class 3 No.82004 seen here at Bath Green Park with the 10.10 to Bristol Temple Meads train in 1964. (*Bob Weaver*)

(*below*) Steam is now coming to an end at Bath Green Park station, as can be seen with the DMU in the platform. The finger destination boards will soon be a thing of the past. Fortunately this station is still there and can be enjoyed and remembered by the many passengers and staff who were part of this once proud railway. (*Keith Barrett collection*)

A wonderful turn of the century photograph taken at Bath Green Park station. It looks like all the railway staff from the station are there. A couple of mysteries need to be explained. The policeman looks like he has a flag in his hand and why is he there? And the garden on the left appears to have ornamental animals in it. (*John Yeo collection*)

Gary Brooker MBE

Gary Brooker is a world-renowned musician and singer and a founder member of the well-known group Procol Harum who had that wonderful hit record *A Whiter Shade of Pale*. He has worked with Eric Clapton, Ringo Starr and Bill Wyman, amongst others, and still tours today to sell-out audiences all around the world. He received his MBE in recognition of his charitable services.

* * *

Being of 'a certain age', I can well remember the sound of gigantic iron wheels slipping on the track, or the slow acceleration of puffing steam as a train left a station, and the immense power of a passenger express going past at full steam.

Growing up in Enfield in Middlesex, trains were all around and a part of daily life. My father led the orchestra in residence at the Palace Hotel in Southend-on-Sea. My holidays were spent there after a journey from Enfield Town to Seven Sisters, there alighting to walk across the road to South Tottenham Station, where we joined the train from St. Pancras via Walthamstow, Barking and Tilbury, eventually reaching our destination at Southend Central; all of this journey done sitting in a lovely warm carriage with the hubbub of London in the 1950s passing by my wide eyes as the smoke and sparks flew by the window.

I was reminded of the 'aroma' of those days of steam when I visited the Watercress Line in Hampshire recently and realised that the pollution in urban areas then was a part of life, and getting from home to your Auntie's house was just a couple of stops and a short, safe walk for a six-year-old.

I used to collect the names and numbers of all the locomotives that I saw, as did most kids then – all the locos seemed to be black or green – I never saw a blue one like on the early Somerset & Dorset Railway which this fine book by Alan and Christine is all about.

My last memory of a steam train journey was on a holiday to Cornwall when I was 12 years old and the line went along the seashore at Dawlish in Devon. I saw palm trees, the sandy beach, and people paddling with knotted handkerchiefs on their heads (perhaps 1957 was a hot summer!). And then I discovered Rock & Roll – music took over, and the railways disappeared.

photograph by Darren Edwards

I count myself really lucky to have grown up in the 50s & 60s, an era when children were left to play games in the parks and streets, and nothing was taken for granted, not even the wondrous design and engineering of the railways of Great Britain.

Oh yes – and of course – then there was Elvis Presley!

The Dorset Central Railway and Extensions Cole to Bournemouth

John Simms

The original Dorset Central route was fairly flat for most of its length and where the trains were running on double-track lines the express engines could work their trains up to 70 or 80 miles per hour. This also explains why the railway enthusiast press carried fewer photographs of the southern section of the mainline. Photographers could not get ahead of the trains to take more than one shot.

Not that the southern section of the line was without its difficulties. There was an awkward climb up Parkstone Bank and keeping the trains moving on the single-line sections when things were busy was as awkward here as everywhere else.

But worst of all was Templecombe. This was one of those locations that fascinated railway enthusiasts and produced more than its fair share of tri-nitro profanity from passengers and staff. Essentially the S&D passed under the London and South Western main line to Exeter but apart from a single, little used, platform there was no Somerset and Dorset station. Instead northbound trains ran under the Exeter line, stopped and waited whilst an engine was attached to the rear of the train, and then reversed into the main station to pick up and set down its passengers. Once this had been done they resumed their journey. Southbound trains ran into the station, the second engine went on the rear and then the whole assemblage had to reverse out and detach that second engine before setting off again.

Some of the main passenger trains did not stop at Templecombe (which has never been more than a large village/small town) but for those which did it was a source of delays and frustration. This was no reflection on the staff who were as efficient as the rest of the 'Dorset' – had they been inefficient the whole system between Bath and Bournemouth would soon

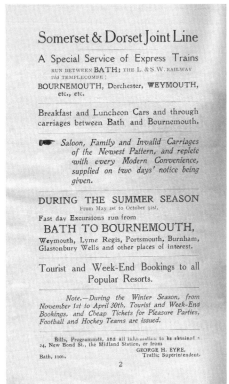

A 1906 advertisement from the 'Borough' Guide to Bath.

have collapsed – but the layout was an absurdity that had grown up piecemeal. So why was it never changed?

Proposals were put forward from time to time but railways have always been an expensive business and for most of the year the delays were to slow local trains. The expresses could run through on the low level without stopping. When it became a major operational embarrassment was on the summer Saturdays when if the shunting in and out of the locals was delayed one soon saw trains standing at signals for miles in each direction. The priority for the rebuilding was never high enough but again it fatally precluded any attempts at speeding services up when rival forms of transport came along.

Again the southern section of the Somerset and Dorset had its railway families who worked for several generations until the closure came and whose part in the local community could work wonders for 'public relations' when things did go awry. It is, after all, much harder to rant at your neighbour rather than one of the faceless 'them'.

When the country railways closed and the railwaymen went to other jobs much irreplaceable experience and goodwill went with them. After March 1966 the last section from Blandford Forum stayed open for freight and the occasional special trains for enthusiasts came and went until the decline in wagon load traffic saw this remaining part of the route closing.

But as the 21st century has dawned revival is under way on one small part of the one-time Dorset Central Railway as a dedicated group has set about refurbishing Shillingstone station. Hopefully this new generation of country railwaymen will bring as much to the local community as their predecessors did.

(*left*) The delight of early summer at Cole, as fireman Ronald Bath takes a break in the warm sunshine on 7F 2-8-0 No.53805, c.1955. (*Ivo Peters, by courtesy of Julian Peters*)

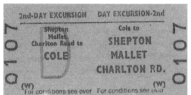

(*right*) Enjoying a rest on Standard 4 No.76025 before continuing their journey on the Dorset, are driver Percy Hobbs (left) and fireman Dick Isaacs, c.1960s. (*Peter Morton*)

(*left*) A scene soon to disappear, as the Highbridge Milky with GWR class 2251 No.2204 in front has just passed Cole signalbox with a down train. (*SDRT collection*)

(*right*) Passing Wincanton on Sunday 6 March 1966 is the down SLS Last Day Special with class 8F No. 48706 in harness with Standard class 4 Tank No.80043. (*Len Taylor*)

(*left*) On a Western Hymek diesel demolition train No.D7003 at Wincanton in 1967 are driver Jack Hobbs and an unknown visitor. It must have been a very sad time for Jack seeing the track being ripped up. (*SDRT collection*)

(*right*) On the outskirts of Wincanton an unidentified 2-10-0 9F with a passenger train makes a fine action shot in the heart of the Somerset countryside. (*Len Taylor*)

This classic scene near Horsington is the 16.13 Evercreech Junction to Templecombe train with driver Percy Hobbs in the cab of 2P No.40509 on 13 August 1955.
(*E.W.Fry/R.K.Blencowe collection*)

On Templecombe shed in 1957 is shed chargeman Doug Barnard and driver Trevor Nettley, who is preparing to do some shunting with 7F No.53801. In the background is fireman John Ceaser on class 2P No.40634 which is waiting to be coaled. (*L.G.Marshall/R.K.Blencowe collection*)

(*above*) Making a fine view with the pleasant Somerset countryside on the right is 2-6-2T class 2 No.41208 standing in Templecombe No.3 platform in February 1965. (*Paul Strong*)

(*below*) A view, looking north, of the railway bridge which carries the SR mainline (Waterloo-Exeter) at Templecombe. Walking with his stick is local shopkeeper Jack Knight, behind him is permanent way man George Belbin and on the right is Councillor Charlie Goddard. (*Ian Matthews collection*)

Charlie Robinson

I started work on the railway as a porter at Templecombe station in 1956. The stationmaster was Bill Newman; other station staff included inspectors Bert Moody, Charles Dicker and Bill Fishleigh. Leading porters I recall were Frank Stiling and Don Garrett and other porters were Trevor Jeans, Stan Newport, Len Rose, Stan May, David Rendle, John Polden and Ron Fudge.

I can recall a few incidents. I remember poor old Bert Moody once opening a livestock wagon one day to give a bull some water; it gave him the fright of his life as it escaped from the wagon. It was found in a field by the main line looking after some cows.

The last train on a Saturday we called the honeymoon special. We knew the honeymoon couples were on board by the blinds being drawn – in those days a lot of the carriages had no corridors.

There was a farmer called Ralph Hayter; he would come and fetch horses in his Austin A35 van. He fed the ropes through the back of the van and would go through the village with the horses trotting along behind. He also brought hay in for the cows and bulls in the cattle wagons. The goods trains often carried cows, sheep, goats and calves. One day a goat was put in with all the luggage, it felt a bit hungry and ate all the luggage labels. Another time on the main line there was a very large wagon with some elephants in it with their keeper. The wagon was rocking from side to side. I'm glad I wasn't in there. Complete farms were often moved by rail from one farm to another.

I recall the farmer who Doris Longman lodged with had a donkey. We asked her how you could tell the age of this donkey. Doris replied: 'It must be old because it has long ears'. Doris worked in Templecombe station buffet with Dolly Sanger and Joan Miles.

One night, shunter Norman Barter cycled from his home in Milborne Port to go to work at Templecombe. It was pitch dark and as he was going through a hamlet called Bowden, a donkey stuck his head over the hedge and went HEE-HAW, HEE-HAW. It frightened him so much he fell off his bike and went over a hedge. He took a bit of ribbing from the lads at the depot about this.

In those days Templecombe was a very busy station and there was always something happening. I remember closing a door on a guards van and it fell off just missing my foot.

Summer time was full of holidaymakers, extra trains were laid on and there was never a spare minute.

At Christmas time we had parcel trains to be sorted and on one occasion some of the parcels had come undone. I was in the office with porter Arthur Bray when inspector Ted Tolley came in and asked what I was repacking. I replied: 'Balls'. Arthur burst out laughing and Ted went on his way. I was re-packing baubles for Christmas trees.

One job I had was to release racing pigeons, which came in on a pigeon special. We released them from the marshalling yard and sometimes outside the station. It was an ideal spot as there were no overhead wires.

Porter Charlie Robinson has just released some racing pigeons outside Templecombe station. In the background is taxi driver Bill Watts, who is giving Charlie a hand. (*Charlie Robinson collection*)

There was a racing tipster called Prince Monolulu, he came down on the main line to go to Wincanton races. He was always dressed in his national costume and would say to everybody: 'I've got a horse, I've got a horse'. Wincanton was also a busy station; there were sidings for the Cow and Gate milk factory, a cattle market and a slaughterhouse.

One time I did a stint of nights at Common Lane Level Crossing at Templecombe. I was informed that two cars would be back at about 9.30pm. After they came back I put the gates across the road, as there was nothing else to do. I went on to be a relief signalman working a few boxes over the S&D.

I enjoyed my life on the Somerset & Dorset Railway and came in contact with many grades of railwaymen like Jim Cull, Bill Butler, Reg Day, my brother Eddie, Stan Flood, Eric Knight, Ralph Gray and Bill Watts.

(*left*) Signalman George Hitchcock poses in the 1960s inside Templecombe station signalbox. It looks extremely clean as did most of the boxes on the railway. George worked at Templecombe for over ten years.

(*right*) The interior of the same signalbox. The block instrument box is being replaced by a signal and telegraph worker, who was probably from Exeter. (*both photographs George Hitchcock collection*)

(*right*) Charlie Robinson making his way back from the sidings where he has been cleaning out some carriages. At the back of the photo can be seen Templecombe carriage and wagon works. (*Charlie Robinson collection*)

(*left*) Guard Albert (Dickie) Bird looks majestic in his railway uniform in this photograph taken in the early 1940s at Templecombe. Dickie was a very keen rose grower, and won many competitions. (*Maureen Carroll collection*)

(*right*) Looking down from the platform on the up Southern main line at Templecombe in 1964, the photograph captures top link driver Ray Stokes cycling to work. Note his railway box on the front of the bike. (*Peter Morton*)

(*above*) Steamraiser Ern Cawley (left) and coalman Frank Ray smile for the camera next to Ivatt Tank No.41206 at Temple-combe shed. (*Keith Barrett collection*)

(*above*) Ticket collector Cecil Gillman is collecting tickets from four young lads who have alighted from a train at Templecombe station. (*Ian Matthews collection*)

B.R.O. 59035

L.M.S. & Southern Rly. Co.'s
(S. and D. Joint Committee)

Via Templecombe and Southern Rly.

(*below*) A photograph of six station staff taken at Templecombe in the early 1900s. Back row, from left to right, Bert Budden, Harry Rose and Harold Milton. Front row, from left to right, Cecil Gillman, Jack Burt and Ted Thomas. (*Ian Matthews collection*)

(*below*) Steamraiser George Merchant (left) and coalman Ern Cawley enjoy a picture to-gether by the coal crane at Templecombe shed. (*Ian Matthews collection*)

(*above*) A view of Templecombe shed. Nearest the camera is SR class G6 No.30274, a 3F Bulldog, and a 7F. The stone building on the left is the old Dorset Central station. On the skyline is the line to Templecombe Upper station. (*Ian Matthews collection*)

(*below*) 7F No.53807 is partly on the turntable at Templecombe in 1960, as George Merchant handles the crane to fill the tender up with coal on the 2-8-0. On the footplate is fireman Pat Holmes, a real S&D character. (*Keith Barrett collection*)

(*above*) Piloting a Bournemouth train back into Templecombe Upper station is Ivatt Tank No.41307. In the background is the MPD and the farthest track is the line to Stalbridge. Who is the lad sitting on the fence enjoying the scene? (*Ian Matthews collection*)

(*below*) A photograph looking north at Templecombe shed in July 1957. Berthed in the yard is 7F No.53800 and Ivatt Tank No.41296. In the distance are Templecombe No.2 signalbox and a Bulleid Pacific running downhill on the single track to Stalbridge. (*Ian Matthews collection*)

(*left*) A photograph of staff with an unidentified 7F taken in 1932 at lower yard, Templecombe. From left to right are driver Fred Mullett, firemen Walt Jeans, Alfie Deer, Den Norris, fitter Stan Good, steamraiser George Merchant and cleaner Reg Pitman. (*Ian Matthews collection*)

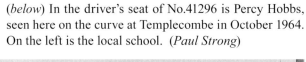

(*right*) Looking out of the cab of Jinty No.47542 is fireman Keith Barrett, seen here at 5.25pm beside the West End shunters' cabin at top yard, Templecombe in 1959. (*Ian Matthews collection*)

(*below*) An unusual sight on the S&D with a DMU near Templecombe Lower working a Birmingham to Bournemouth excursion train on 25 May 1958. (*C.L. Caddy*)

(*below*) In the driver's seat of No.41296 is Percy Hobbs, seen here on the curve at Templecombe in October 1964. On the left is the local school. (*Paul Strong*)

(*right*) An interesting view in 1961 of a trio of 2P locos Nos. 40634, 40563 and 40569 leaving Templecombe for assisting duties at Evercreech Junction. (*Wally Arnott collection*)

(*below*) Reversing back into the engine shed at Templecombe is driver Rodney Scovell with Standard class 5 No.73087, *Linette*, c.1961. (*Keith Barrett collection*)

(*below*) Arriving back on Templecombe shed is driver George Welch and fireman Clifford Day with a class 7F No.53803 in 1959. (*Keith Barrett collection*)

A very rare photograph of Templecombe No.3 Junction (Horsington) signalbox with the bobby looking out of the window. Members of the permanent way, all with white shirts on, are posing for the camera. If you look closely, pot plants are on the windowledges and the veranda. This box was opened in February 1902 as a replacement for the earlier box, and was closed in February 1933. The area was then taken over by No.2 Junction signalbox. On the right can be seen the gates for Horsington Crossing. (*Jim Milton collection*)

(*left*) Putting on steam is an unidentified Pannier Tank going bunker first with a Sunday milk train for Bailey Gate in January 1965. (*Paul Strong*)

(*right*) One of the best known names on the Somerset & Dorset Railway was footplateman Johnny Walker. He joined the railway at Bath Green Park in 1921 and spent all his working life on the railway, ending. There was many a story he could tell about the S&D (see *Stories of the Somerset & Dorset* for reminiscences of incidents around Stalbridge and Sturminster Newton) and none of his fellow crewmen had a bad word to say about him. (*Authors' collection*)

(*left*) Quite an event for the children having their photograph taken at Henstridge station in the early 1900s. They all look very smart. We wonder where they are going? A lady on the left is also posing for the camera. (*SDRT collection*)

(*right*) It's a year before closure, but the Stalbridge station staff haven't let the station run down. Freshly painted lines on the platform and painted stones around the flower beds are all part of the pride they felt about their railway. In the platform is 2-6-4T class 4 No.80059 with a mixed train. (*Paul Strong*)

(*left*) In May 1965 the signalman, who looks like Robert (Jock) McKennie, is ready to exchange the tablet with the fireman of a Standard Tank as it runs into Stalbridge with an up local. Waiting in the down loop is Standard class 4 No.75073 with a goods train. (*Paul Strong*)

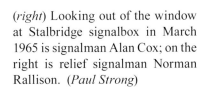

(*right*) Looking out of the window at Stalbridge signalbox in March 1965 is signalman Alan Cox; on the right is relief signalman Norman Rallison. (*Paul Strong*)

What an absolutely stunning photograph taken in the bad winter of 1963. The view from Bonslea House, Sturminster Newton looks across the frozen River Stour as a train heads for Stalbridge. (*Helmut Eckardt*)

Haymaking in progress makes a superb view from Gain's Cross looking towards Shillingstone, as a six-coach passenger train is seen in the distance, c.1930s. (*Gwyn Rogers collection*)

(*above*) Pictured here are members of the station staff and a young puppy at Sturminster Newton in the early 1900s. William Henry Owen, pictured here in the middle of the front row, was stationmaster at this station for over 41 years. In 1921 he was obliged to resign his position through ill health. Such was the respect and goodwill of the community towards him that an illuminated address was commissioned for him by 143 subscribers on 27 November 1921. He was also given a cheque for 60 guineas. (*Sturminster Newton Museum*)

(*below*) Troops waiting at Sturminster Newton station during World War 1. We wonder how many of the brave lads came back to their loved ones? (*Sturminster Newton Museum*)

(*above*) This has to be one of my all-time favourite photographs of S&D staff. This is the last track permanent way gang for the section between Sturminster Newton (where this picture was taken) and Blandford. The gang are certainly enjoying their scrumpy and who is holding who up? In the gang are, from left to right, Jack Newman, Billy Ware, Denzil (Digger) Curtis, Duchey Mullens, Albert Snook and Harry Guy. (*Gwyn Rogers*)

(*below*) On 7 March 1966 the S&D was finally closed for passenger traffic. This brought to an end 103 years of rail travel at Sturminster Newton. This photograph shows an SLS special hauled by 8F No.48706 and Standard 4 Tank No.80043 at the station with local people of all ages saying their goodbyes. (*Helmut Eckardt*)

(*above*) Shopping is on the cards for a trip to Bournemouth for these ladies at Sturminster Newton station. Waiting for the train are left to right, Mary Clacy, Mrs. Winifred Harnett and her friend Miss Margaret Richardson, c.1960s. (*Geoff & Mary Clacy collection*)

(*left*) A sad occasion, but a nice photo of Sturminster Newton residents in front of the signalbox on the last day of train services through their station in March 1966. In the group are, from left to right, Ray Rogers, Simon Rogers, Susan Caines, Fred Clarke, Miss Wallis, Mrs. Wallis and Mrs. Clarke. (*Gwyn Rogers*)

(*below right*) A wonderful photograph of Sturminster Newton stationmaster William Henry Owen, c.1900s, standing outside his home, which stills exists today, now known as Ivy Cottage. (*Sturminster Newton Museum*)

(*below left*) Station staff at Sturminster Newton in the 1930s. On the right is porter Walt (Sticker) Fudge who was renowned for being first in the queue for getting tips off the passengers. (*Sturminster Newton Museum*)

(*left*) Plenty of activity here as a Pannier Tank is about to pass Shillingstone signalbox with a northbound train while a local train for Bournemouth sits in the other platform. (*SDRT collection*)

(*right*) Signalman Bert Scammell with his brand new bike at Shillingstone station is waiting to catch the 12.52 to Blandford Forum where he worked as a signalman. His brother Harry was a relief signalman on the S&D. (*Bob Downes*)

(*left*) This was the last summer before Dr. Beeching closed the Somerset & Dorset Railway. BR Standard 5 No.73001 is the locomotive power on this Bank Holiday Special in August 1965. The enthusiasts at Shillingstone are enjoying their day out and the cameras are snapping the occasion. Looking out of the cab is young fireman John Sawyer; his driver for the day was Ben Ford. (*Peter Morton*)

Ron Jeans

My first memories of the S&D were coming to Durweston in the 1930s to visit my grandparents. I spent many happy school holidays with them. They lived at France Hill cottages just a few yards from the line. At 9.40am the first train from Bath came through on its way to Bournemouth. At 10.20am the Pines Express, with its majestic Midland coaches, came up the Milldown incline. It then gathered speed for its journey to Manchester and Sheffield. At the head of the train was a 4-4-0 locomotive, on its tender in bold lettering it had LMS. During the summer holidays this train was double-headed. Then in 1938 the new Black Five 4-6-0 engines arrived to take over the Pines, an impressive sight.

My first journey on the S&D was from Blandford to Stourpaine and Durweston Halt. This was after my suggestion to my mother that this would be a great treat as we usually travelled out on the Hants and Dorset bus. The next trip I remember was from Stourpaine and Durweston Halt to Poole where I saw Father Christmas for the first time. The years passed until in 1942 I came to work in Durweston, travelling by train only when necessary, as it was standing room all the way.

The first August Saturday Bank Holiday in 1946 was a sight to remember at the halt. The 1.00pm train was running one hour late, the locomotive was a T9 4-4-0 of the Southern Railway, hauling 10 coaches. After it stopped it moved forward twice to let the passengers off. It struggled to get the train moving again.

I recall a train that made a special stop for pupils of Durweston Primary School for a trip to London; the halt had a porter in attendance for that day. It may be interesting to note that the engine from Bournemouth was a West Country class No.34107 *Blandford Forum*. The following year a 10-coach school special stopped at the halt picking up its first passengers of the day for Portsmouth Harbour station, at its head was gleaming West Country No.34042 *Dorchester*. It seemed it had just come out of the works. When it returned, these were the very last passengers to alight at the halt. As it pulled out, the glare from the firebox was shining in the evening twilight as it headed for Shillingstone, a magnificent sight.

Durweston and the old S&D has been an important part of my life, so when it closed in March 1966 it was a very sad time. I made my last journey on the line on 5 March. I arrived at Blandford station just before 2.00pm with my three sons and a nephew. We purchased day returns for the 2.05pm to Templecombe. As we were travelling round the curve at Nutford, through the

This postcard shows the first train to stop at Stourpaine and Durweston Halt in July 1928 and what an occasion for the local people. The motive power is a Johnson 0-4-4T. The platform was 120 feet long, made of concrete and situated on the down side of the line. It closed to traffic in September 1956. (*Authors' collection*)

cutting at France Farm, someone in our compartment exclaimed: 'It is surprising how we all turn out for the funeral'. Then I realised, yes, we were attending the last day of timetabled passenger service of the Somerset & Dorset Railway.

Alighting at Templecombe we proceeded to the yard to be greeted by the shedmaster Harry Jeans: 'We haven't much for you to see as everything must leave the branch today'. Two locos with connecting rods removed were on their way to the scrap yard at Ringwood. Then we came across an 8F in steam. After enquiries I found out it was making its last journey to Bath. We went back to the station and bought our tickets for the 4.18pm to Bath. The train comprised three carriages, which were full. After a while we became worried about how we were going to return home, but the guard assured us that he was returning with the last service train from Bath at 6.10pm.

Arriving at Bath was utter chaos, we had to stay put in the compartment as we were packed in like sardines and couldn't get out. We left Bath with the sound of detonators and made our way to Templecombe. On arrival we were hungry and thirsty so we had some refreshments on Templecombe station. Out on the platform there were crowds of people who were wishing to travel, or just saying farewell to the S&D. Many of the passengers who had travelled from Bath were now boarding for the last train back to Bath. This was double-headed with the leading engine carrying a wreath on the smokebox door; what a send-off.

Next it was our turn to leave. Before boarding, we said farewell to the shedmaster and the guard who had given a lifetime of service to the railway. Now we were leaving on the last service train to Bournemouth. As we were reversing out of the station the local landlord, Pat Dorland, was playing the last post on the bugle. Then with exploding detonators and waves from local inhabitants we were on our way to Blandford, stopping at Henstridge, Stalbridge, Sturminster Newton and Shillingstone. All the local people came out to witness the last train and the passing of the old S&D. It was now approaching 9.30pm on a very clear, frosty night with a full moon. We came through the cutting at Gains Cross and Durweston came into view, which was my home village. With a tear in my eye we passed the disused halt and the driver gave a blast on the whistle as he had done so many times that evening. The distant came into view, then we braked for Blandford. We alighted, by now very tired, but stayed as the engine was filled with water. Blandford railwayman, Ivor Ridout, told us they were holding up the train as long as they could, so everybody could say their final goodbyes. Then with exploding detonators it left the station and disappeared from view; the feeling of sadness I shall never forget.

The heavy powerful Standard 5 No.73001 with the up mail is seen here on a clear Dorset day at Nutford Farm, Stourpaine, in the 1960s. Note the GWR coach third from the back. (*Ron Jeans*)

147

(*above*) BR class 4 Tank No.80019 energetically runs around at Blandford Forum. Even after closure the staff have kept the station neat and tidy. (*Paul Strong*)

(*below*) Parcels are being loaded in to the van as Standard 4 No.76015 waits patiently before heading southbound to Bournemouth. (*SDRT collection*)

(*right*) On the up platform at Blandford Forum looking north. On the left is the porter's room with a barrow and mace sacks and four other wheeled trolleys. Behind them is Bridge House which was occupied by the Brickell family in the 1960s. The iron bridge is still in situ today. Stationmaster Albert Powis, on the right, is talking to foreman Henry Hall. (*Jack Powis collection*)

(*left*) Health and safety would have had a field day with the number of people on the track taking photos of Ivatt 2-6-2T No.41320 at Blandford Forum on 25 March 1967. (*SDRT collection*)

(*right*) Blandford shunter Ivor (Ginger) Ridout is in front of No. 80019, making his way towards the Bournemouth Central guard, who is on the trackbed next to his guard's van. Sadly, Ivor is no longer with us; he was a wonderful S&D character and a fine railwayman. This photograph was taken after closure of the line. (*Paul Strong*)

(*left*) Even though this halt was hardly ever used, this photograph looking south shows Charlton Marshall Halt surprisingly well looked after in 1964. (*Keith Barrett collection*)

(*right*) It's shirt sleeve weather at Bailey Gate, as the enthusiasts enjoy their day out on a LCGB Rail Tour in 1960, with one of the 2-8-0s No.53804 at the head of the train. On the left-hand side is United Dairies Milk Factory, formerly Carters & Dorset Modern Dairies. (*Keith Barrett collection*)

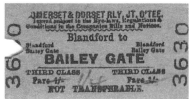

(*left*) 4-6-0 Standard 5 No.73051 makes steady progress with a mixed train at Bailey Gate. These locos were introduced in 1951 and designed at Doncaster. (*SDRT collection*)

(*right*) Having just come off the single line at Corfe Mullen, class 7F No.53802 runs at speed northwards with an up local working in 1955. (*SDRT collection*)

(*left*) A dramatic shot of Bulldog 0-6-0 No.76 with a goods train at Corfe Mullen. This loco was built at Neilson Reid & Co in 1902 and worked for 47 years before being withdrawn. (*Keith Barrett collection*)

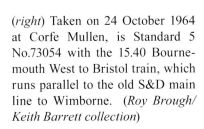

(*right*) Taken on 24 October 1964 at Corfe Mullen, is Standard 5 No.73054 with the 15.40 Bournemouth West to Bristol train, which runs parallel to the old S&D main line to Wimborne. (*Roy Brough/ Keith Barrett collection*)

(*left*) Seen here at Wimborne in all its glory is a small Johnson 4-4-0 No.68 built at Derby in 1896. Wimborne was closed to S&D passenger trains in 1920 and to goods trains in 1933. (*Keith Barrett collection*)

(*below*) Looking out of the cab of 4F No.43912 at Broadstone is driver Bert Brewer. Bert was based at Branksome and on one occasion he lost his teeth whilst looking out of the cab. The story goes that they were found by a member of the permanent way gang and returned to him in a smart box tied with a bow. (*Keith Barrett collection*)

(*right*) Standing at Broadstone are U class No.31639 and West Country class No.34015 *Exmouth* waiting to work an RCTS special over the S&D line on 2 January 1966. (*Keith Barrett collection*)

(*left*) This 4F No.44102, seen here at Broadstone, could do with a day with the cleaners, as she pulls a rake of open wagons with the Evercreech Junction to Hamworthy goods in February 1960. (*M.K. Lewis/Keith Barrett collection*)

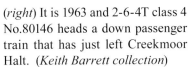

(*right*) It is 1963 and 2-6-4T class 4 No.80146 heads a down passenger train that has just left Creekmoor Halt. (*Keith Barrett collection*)

(*left*) It is the big freeze of 1963 and it looks bitterly cold at Holes Bay Junction, Poole, as 4F No.44411 provides the motive power for the 13.10 Bournemouth West to Bristol train in January of that year. (*Keith Barrett collection*)

(*right*) With the floodlights of Poole stadium on the left a Stanier class 5 No.45333 departs with the evening goods for Bath via the S&D in 1964. (*Roy Brough/Keith Barrett collection*)

(*left*) Ivatt class 2 No.41243 at Parkstone, pulling the 12.23 Templecombe to Bournemouth West three-coach passenger train on 27 April 1964. (*Keith Barrett collection*)

(*left*) A view of Bulldog 0-6-0 No.62 on Branksome turntable. The loco was built in 1896, later her LMS number was 3194, and under BR the number changed to 43194. She was finally withdrawn in 1960. (*Tim Deacon collection*)

(*right*) Steaming freely at Branksome is Black Five No.45333 on a northbound evening goods to Bath. (*Roy Brough/Keith Barrett collection*)

(*left*) In thick snow and looking a bit worse for wear, is 4F No.44167 at Branksome shed in 1963. The loco has a Templecombe shed code (82G). (*Keith Barrett collection*)

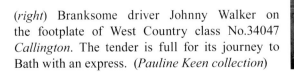

(*right*) Branksome driver Johnny Walker on the footplate of West Country class No.34047 *Callington*. The tender is full for its journey to Bath with an express. (*Pauline Keen collection*)

(*above*) A line-up of wonderful vintage motor cars at Bournemouth West terminus in 1930. This station must have been a fine sight to the holidaymakers arriving for their summer holidays from the north. (*Richard Dagger collection*)

(*below*) Pushing its stock back into the carriage sidings at Bournemouth West is Standard class 5 No.73088 *Joyous Gard* at Whitsun in 1965. (*Peter Morton*)

(*right*) 4F No.44560 (ex-SDJR No.60) seen at Bournemouth West as it reverses out to the carriage sidings with the 12.23 Templecombe to Bournemouth West train. (*Keith Barrett collection*)

(*left*) A Bath-bound train stands at Bournemouth West on 30 June 1946. The locomotive for the trip north is Stanier class 5MT No.4805. (*Keith Barrett collection*)

(*right*) The sun is shining brightly at Bournemouth Central in 1964, as 4F No.44558 and 7F No.53807 are seen prior to working a special over the Somerset & Dorset. (*Keith Barrett collection*)

Index

160